Imagining the TENTH Dimension

a new way of thinking about time and space

by Rob Bryanton

Talking Dog
www.talkingdogstudios.com
Published by Talking Dog Studios, Inc.

Bryanton, Rob, 1954–
Imagining the Tenth Dimension / Rob Bryanton

First published in Canada June 2006 by Talking Dog Studios, Inc.

Production Credits
Typesetting/layout by Rob Bryanton
Illustrations for book & tenth dimension.com website by Jason Orban, OH! Media
Website design for tenth dimension.com by TrentHaus/JasonOrban, OH! Media
Contact OH! Media at www.ohmedia.ca
Contact the author at rob@tenthdimension.com
For discussion group and further info, go to www.tenthdimension.com

Note for Librarians: A cataloguing record for this book is available from Library and Archives Canada at www.collectionscanada.ca/amicus/index-e.html
ISBN 1-4251-0380-4

Printed on paper with minimum 30% recycled fibre.
Trafford's print shop runs on "green energy" from solar, wind and other environmentally-friendly power sources.

TRAFFORD
PUBLISHING™
Offices in Canada, USA, Ireland and UK

Book sales for North America and international:
Trafford Publishing, 6E–2333 Government St.,
Victoria, BC V8T 4P4 CANADA
phone 250 383 6864 (toll-free 1 888 232 4444)
fax 250 383 6804; email to orders@trafford.com
Book sales in Europe:
Trafford Publishing (UK) Limited, 9 Park End Street, 2nd Floor
Oxford, UK OX1 1HH UNITED KINGDOM
phone 44 (0)1865 722 113 (local rate 0845 230 9601)
facsimile 44 (0)1865 722 868; info.uk@trafford.com
Order online at:
trafford.com/06-2137

10 9 8 7 6 5 4 3

To Gail, Todd and Mark:
my family, my debating team, my friends.

TABLE OF CONTENTS

Preamble

The "theory of reality" that I advance in this book and on the website www.tenthdimension.com is not the one that is commonly accepted by today's physicists. Anyone wanting to know more about the currently established thinking behind string theory and the tenth or eleventh dimension should refer to such excellent books as "Parallel Worlds" by Michio Kaku, "The Fabric of the Cosmos" by Brian Greene, or "Warped Passages" by Lisa Randall.

I invite you to think of this as an entertaining diversion that for some people will have a strong and thought-provoking connection to their impression of how the world really works. A discussion forum at www.tenthdimension.com gives readers an opportunity to debate the concepts presented in these pages more fully.

Enjoy!

Rob Bryanton
June 2006

INTRODUCTION

Our universe is an amazing and humbling place. The planet we live on is filled with wondrous things, yet it is only an unimaginably tiny part of the cosmos. As our knowledge expands up beyond galaxies and down to the quarks and neutrinos, we pass through one incomprehensibly large order of magnitude after another, dwarfing us with the complexity of it all.

Now we have string theory adding yet another layer to the mystery. Reality, today's physicists tell us, is based upon the resonances of exquisitely small "superstrings" vibrating in something called the tenth dimension. This is a concept the average person simply has no way to deal with. Tiny strings creating reality? And how can there even *be* ten dimensions? Most of us have barely gotten used to the idea of there being four.

The goal of this text is to provide the tools that will allow us to imagine the construction of ten dimensions. Along the way, we'll discuss a number of other mysteries, including the huge amount of Dark Matter and Dark Energy missing from the universe, quantum indeterminacy, and consciousness. This exploration will be based upon some of the current theories of reality being advanced by modern physics, but it will also introduce ways of looking at the relationship between physical space and time which fall outside the generally accepted viewpoint.

As an aside, anyone wanting to know more about the science behind superstrings and the tenth dimension[1] would do well to refer to such books as "Parallel Worlds" by Michio Kaku, or Brian Greene's "The Fabric of the Cosmos". These books (as we already mentioned in the Preamble) introduce us to the people and science that led to superstrings becoming the current dominant theory of the nature of reality. These authors are also not afraid to deal with the more "out there" ramifications of modern physics, and sprinkle these books with fanciful examples from modern fiction and pop culture, creating eminently readable texts. Another recommended book is "Warped Passages" by Lisa Randall: an enlightening exploration of string theory and advanced topics such as branes, supersymmetry, and the duality of the tenth and eleventh dimensions. The tone of Randall's book is a bit more serious, although it too has a certain amount of whimsy.

To be absolutely clear about this, the explanation of the ten dimensions you will find in these pages is not contained within the works of experts such as Kaku, Greene, or Randall, nor is it intended to imply that they would somehow endorse the conclusions about to be explored. Let me say from the outset that I realize the basic geometry concepts used in chapter one to arrive at my description of the ten dimensions will seem very simple indeed when compared to the challenging formulas and topologies used by string theorists in their research. Despite that, I would ask the reader to keep an open mind: sometimes, simple is better. I will argue in these pages that this "simple" viewpoint has many fascinating connections, not just to leading-edge string theory and physics, but also to the

---

[1] (as well as the eleventh dimension, which we'll also touch upon in these pages)

average person's common sense knowledge of how the world really works.

Modern science asks us to accept the concept of ten dimensions as a topological construct that is essentially unimaginable to three-dimensional creatures such as ourselves: ten spatial dimensions happen to be where the mathematics of string theory work, and that is something we laymen just have to accept. In past decades there have been indications that the math works quite well in twenty-six dimensions too, but thankfully, that idea is currently not in vogue.

This project began as a set of songs, twenty-six of which you will find referenced throughout this document as endnotes (like the one at the end of this paragraph). Although my "day job" is composing music for television series and films, most of these songs were written over the last twenty years not for shows but for my own personal enjoyment. They revolve around a ten-dimensional "theory of reality" which I, a non-scientist with an inquisitive mind, gradually developed through my own fascination with the hidden structures of the universe now being revealed by modern science. Like many people, I am particularly intrigued by the growing sense that there is a convergence beginning to take place between science and philosophy. Big questions about what is really happening when we perceive ourselves to be experiencing the physical world around us seem to be moving towards parallel conclusions from both camps: these ideas are major themes through this book and within the attached songs. In some cases the song lyrics amplify or provide a parallel commentary to the discussion taking place at that point in the text, while elsewhere they are simply echoing what has already been established. Song lyrics can be very useful for setting up repetitious patterns which help to reinforce an idea. Hopefully these will add an enjoyable diversion to the discussions at hand.[i]

Once I had written these songs, it became apparent that the concepts being presented still needed further explanation to establish the reasoning behind them. For me, science fiction authors such as Greg Bear and Stephen Baxter, whose works tend to have more "science" in their fiction, have been influential as I developed this theory over the last two decades. When I first developed the ideas this book is based upon, it was long before the moment I first heard of string theory. Then, over the years, numerous articles in Scientific American, Discover, Popular Science, and of course the books of Stephen Hawking all began to fascinate me more and more as I saw connections between my own ideas and the theories of quantum physics, multiple dimensions, and then superstrings.

As I began to more seriously research the science behind string theory in the course of writing this book, two things struck me: first, I was surprised to learn that the dimensional construct I am proposing appears to be unique. Secondly, it appears to be quite compatible with what is known as the "Many Worlds Theory" which was first advanced by physicist Hugh Everett III in 1957. The "Many Worlds Theory" is a proposed explanation for the mysterious "particle/wave" nature of subatomic particles. At the risk of oversimplifying, Dr. Everett's theory says that subatomic particles are simultaneously waves and particles because the other potential wave-states for those particles really do exist in a multitude of other universes which are inaccessible to us. In other words, all possible outcomes exist simultaneously in something physicists now call "the multiverse", and the probability wave function of quantum indeterminacy is not a theory but a very real aspect of these mutually unobservable but equally real worlds. Also known as the "Theory of the Universal Wave-function", the Many Worlds Theory has, coincidentally, enjoyed renewed support in the last few years in the world of physicists developing string theory. While many renowned scientists including Stephen Hawking and Richard Feynman have embraced the Many Worlds theory, it also has its opponents in the scientific community who reject it on the grounds that it is "too extravagant".

The thought of any theory of the universe being too extravagant is, to my way of thinking, quite amusing. For the last few years there was a wonderful show in the Rose Center's Hayden Planetarium at New York's American Museum of Natural History, called "Passport to the Universe". Narrated by Tom Hanks, it was a highly effective visual journey which took the viewer through one order of magnitude leap after another, from the earth to the solar system, to our galaxy, to our local group and then our local supercluster of galaxies, and on out to the hundred billion galaxies and seventy sextillion stars (that's 7 followed by 22 zeroes!) currently believed to make up our observable universe. This magnificent presentation would be useful as an introduction to the concepts we are about to explore: anyone wanting to dismiss the levels of detail we are imagining in these pages as "too extravagant" would do well to keep in mind how extraordinarily, inconceivably extravagant we already know the universe to be.

According to the most popular version of string theory, the six higher dimensions above the four we live in are most likely curled up on themselves, unimaginably small, and all around us. According to the current enhancement to string theory known as "M-Theory", there may actually be eleven dimensions, which would include ten spatial dimensions and one dimension of time. New theories like these are revealing surprising dualities where the tenth dimension and the eleventh dimension are in a sense equivalent to each other: this may be a fortuitous coincidence since, in the journey we are about to take, we will contend that the tenth dimension is as far as you need to go.

All of these theories tell us that it is the harmonics of superstring vibrations happening in the tenth spatial dimension that create the basic laws that define our reality—the strength of gravity, the charge, spin and nature of subatomic particles, and so on. It is the energy of these strings' vibrations which is converted into mass (through the logic of Einstein's most famous equation, $E=mc^2$), so strings that have faster vibrations are creating the subatomic particles that have greater mass.

In the following pages we will try to show the ways in which "Imagining the Tenth Dimension" is compatible with the current thinking of string theorists and cosmologists. But whether string theory is ultimately proven to be right or wrong really has no bearing on the journey we are about to take: the ultimate point of this exercise will be that by imagining all ten dimensions, we will have imagined a fabric that can account for all aspects of reality. A tall order! Let's begin.

ONE-A QUICK TOUR OF TEN DIMENSIONS

Most of us are quite familiar with the first four dimensions. We have grown comfortable with the idea that we live in a three-dimensional world, and that time is an additional dimension. We will use the relationships between those first four dimensions to gradually build a mental image of what each succeeding dimension could be like. By taking our imagination through one level at a time, we will arrive at a construct much larger than what we could ever hope to imagine all at once, building one layer upon another until we get to the tenth dimension.

THE FIRST DIMENSION–A LINE

We start with a point. A point, in geometry, has no size, no dimension, it is purely a descriptor which indicates a certain value or location in a system. In other words, a point is just a pointer.

The first dimension, for our purposes, is any straight line joining two points (see Illustration 1).

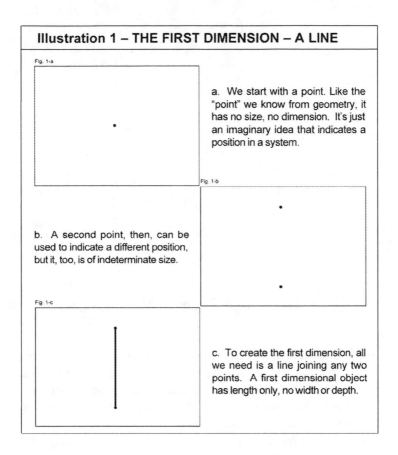

Illustration 1 – THE FIRST DIMENSION – A LINE

Fig. 1-a

a. We start with a point. Like the "point" we know from geometry, it has no size, no dimension. It's just an imaginary idea that indicates a position in a system.

Fig. 1-b

b. A second point, then, can be used to indicate a different position, but it, too, is of indeterminate size.

Fig 1-c

c. To create the first dimension, all we need is a line joining any two points. A first dimensional object has length only, no width or depth.

THE SECOND DIMENSION–A SPLIT

If the first dimension is length, then the second is width. But for this discussion, let's come up with a slightly different way of describing the second dimension.

Let's begin by drawing a straight line. At some point along the line, we'll draw another line that branches off from the first. We should now have drawn a shape that looks something like a simple letter "y". But what we have also drawn is a representation of a two dimensional object.

The first line we drew has only length (or rather it represents only length, for of course if we were to look at the line we drew with a microscope we would see that it has not only length but a good deal of width as well), so that line represents a one-dimensional object. As soon as we had split that straight line in two or branched off to a different line, we entered a representation of the second dimension: the object we've drawn now has length and width (see Illustration 2).

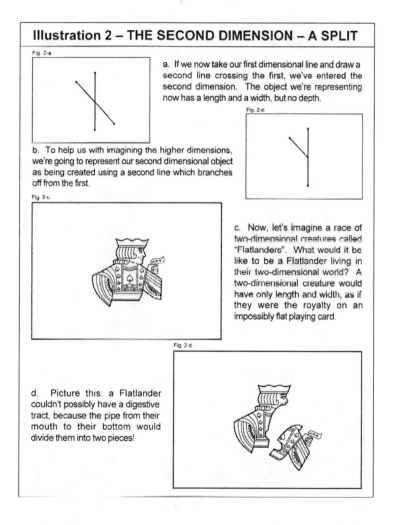

Illustration 2 – THE SECOND DIMENSION – A SPLIT

Fig. 2-a

a. If we now take our first dimensional line and draw a second line crossing the first, we've entered the second dimension. The object we're representing now has a length and a width, but no depth.

Fig. 2-b

b. To help us with imagining the higher dimensions, we're going to represent our second dimensional object as being created using a second line which branches off from the first.

Fig. 2-c

c. Now, let's imagine a race of two-dimensional creatures called "Flatlanders". What would it be like to be a Flatlander living in their two-dimensional world? A two-dimensional creature would have only length and width, as if they were the royalty on an impossibly flat playing card.

Fig. 2-d

d. Picture this: a Flatlander couldn't possibly have a digestive tract, because the pipe from their mouth to their bottom would divide them into two pieces!

Figure 2-e | **Illustration 2 - continued**

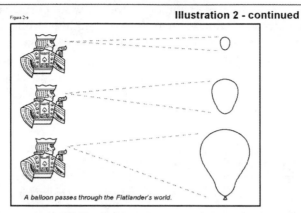

A balloon passes through the Flatlander's world.

e. A Flatlander trying to view our three-dimensional world would only be able to perceive shapes in two-dimensional cross-sections. A balloon, for instance, would start as a tiny dot, become a hollow circle which inexplicably grows to a certain size, then shrinks back to a dot before popping out of existence.

Figure 2-f

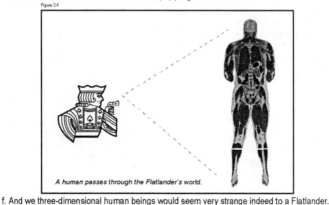

A human passes through the Flatlander's world.

f. And we three-dimensional human beings would seem very strange indeed to a Flatlander.

THE THIRD DIMENSION–A FOLD

A famous book written in 1884 by Edwin Abbott ("Flatland: A Romance of Many Dimensions") described a world of Flatlanders: two-dimensional creatures living in a two-dimensional world. Written under the pseudonym "A Square", the book describes the adventures of A Square in "Lineland" (the first dimension) and "Spaceland" (the third dimension). While the book is an attempt to popularize the notion of multidimensional geometry, it is also commonly described as a clever satire on the social, moral, and religious values of the day.

What would a three dimensional creature such as ourselves look like to a two-dimensional Flatlander? Since they can only perceive two of our three dimensions, they would be able to see us only in cross sections: a Flatlander viewing one of us passing through their Flatland World might first see ten small objects representing our toes, which would become two larger objects which would grow and shrink and grow again as the Flatlander's viewpoint travelled past our feet and up our legs, becoming one large object as they reached our middle, and so on. To a Flatlander, we 3D beings would be able to pop in and out of their two-dimensional world as if by magic, and our texture and form would be quite inexplicable. In the same way, we humans would find the 2D information that a Flatlander sees to be a useless and confusing jumble of lines all in the same plane.

Now picture this. An ant marching from the left to the right side of a newspaper page could be thought of as a Flatlander walking along in a two dimensional world. What if we want to help that ant get to his destination sooner, so we fold the newspaper to make it meet in the middle? Suddenly, the ant is able to finish his cross-paper trek much more quickly and go on his way.

When we folded the paper, we took the representation of a two-dimensional object and moved it through the third dimension. If there had been Flatlanders living on that page, the ant would seem to have suddenly disappeared from one location, and magically reappeared at another.

So, for our purposes, let's call the third dimension what we move through to get from one point to another in the dimension below. Since we are all three dimensional creatures, let's not waste time talking about all the other aspects of what it means to be three dimensional. By using this mental shortcut, imagining dimension three as what we move through to jump from one point in dimension two to another, we have a tool which will be useful in imagining the higher dimensions (see Illustration 3).

One – A Quick Tour of Ten Dimensions

Illustration 3 – THE THIRD DIMENSION – A FOLD

Fig. 3-a

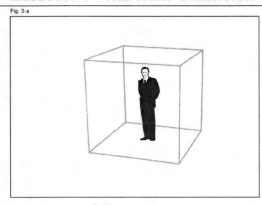

a. Imagining the third dimension is the easiest for us because every moment of our lives that is what we're in. A three dimensional object has length, width, and height.

Fig. 3-b

b. But here's another way to describe the third dimension: if we imagine an ant walking across a newspaper which is lying on a table, we can pretend that the ant is a Flatlander, walking along on a flat two-dimensional newspaper world.

c. If that paper is now folded in the middle, we create a way for our Flatlander Ant to "magically" disappear from one position in his two-dimensional world and be instantly transported to another. We can imagine that we did this by taking a two-dimensional

Fig. 3-c

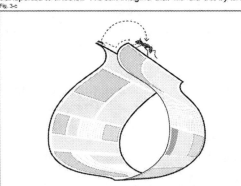

object and folding it through the dimension above, which is our third dimension. Once again, it will be more convenient for us as we imagine the higher dimensions if we can think of the third dimension in this way: the third dimension is what you "fold through" to jump from one point to another in the dimension below.

THE FOURTH DIMENSION–A LINE

Another common way of thinking of each additional dimension is that each is at a right angle to the previous one. That's easy for the first three dimensions–if we have a box, its length (first dimension) is at right angles to its width (second dimension), which is at right angles to its height (third dimension). But what's at right angles to that?

One answer would be–its duration. By now most of us have gotten used to the idea that the fourth dimension can be thought of as time. So here's a concept for you: if you were to imagine yourself as a fourth dimensional creature, you would be like a long undulating snake, with your tiny embryonic self at one end, and your deceased self at the other, and your current self some place between! But because we perceive things in the third dimension, we (in a similar way to the Flatlanders in the dimension below us) only see a three dimensional cross-section of our fourth-dimensional bodies when we look at ourselves in a mirror.

Time is a line which joins (or passes through) two points. But those points are of indeterminate size, which means they can be of any size we choose to imagine them being. So what we are also imagining is that the fourth dimension is what joins the entirety of three-dimensional space to a corresponding but different three-dimensional space elsewhere in time. To say it another way, the universe we are in now is slightly but unquestionably different from the universe we were in one minute ago, and those two universes are separated (or joined) by a line drawn in the fourth dimension, which we call time.

The minor complication is that we experience "time" as a line that moves in one direction only, which is an issue we'll explore more in later chapters. Because of our linear "one-way" experience of time, physicists usually do not pursue the line of reasoning we are embarking upon: instead, they keep "time" as a separate concept from the spatial dimensions they use in their calculations. We are going to argue here that time really is just another spatial dimension, and that the dimensions above it can be easily imagined using that line of reasoning (see Illustration 4).

Illustration 4 – THE FOURTH DIMENSION – A LINE

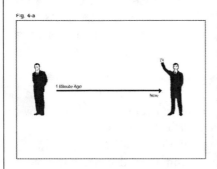

Fig. 4-a

a. The first three dimensions can be described with these words: "length, width, and depth". What word can we assign to the fourth dimension? One answer would be, "duration". If we think of ourselves as we were one minute ago, and then imagine ourselves as we are this moment, the line we could draw from the "one-minute-ago" version of ourselves to the "right now" version would be a line in the fourth dimension.

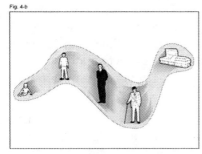

Fig. 4-b

b. If you were to see your body in the fourth dimension, you would be like a long undulating snake, with your embryonic self at one end and your deceased self at the other.

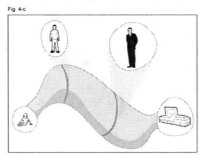

Fig 4-c

c. But because we live from moment to moment in the third dimension, we are like our second-dimensional Flatlanders Just like that Flatlander who could only see two-dimensional cross-sections of objects from the dimension above, we as three-dimensional creatures can only see three-dimensional cross-sections of our fourth-dimensional self.

The idea of "time" being a real spatial dimension is admittedly a very old concept,[2] and one which some readers may have trouble with from the outset because it appears to

---

[2] For instance, this concept was used by science fiction author H.G.Wells over a hundred years ago as his explanation for the operation of "The Time Machine" in his novel of the same name.

be such a hackneyed science fiction cliché. All I can do is ask those readers to please set aside the conclusions they might be jumping to about the usefulness of this text and to continue to examine the line of reasoning being followed.

As we imagine dimensions higher than four, we are going to picture a simple and symmetric cycle that continues to repeat as we move up from one dimension to the next. We saw that we could sum up dimensions one, two, and three as a line, a split, and a fold. If dimension four is a line, what would that mean if dimensions five and six were a split and a fold?

THE FIFTH DIMENSION–A SPLIT

Have you ever made a Möbius strip? Take a long thin strip of paper, add one twist to it, and tape the ends of the strip together, forming a loop. If you now take a pencil and draw along the length of the strip you've created, something surprising happens. By the time your line meets itself along the loop again, you will have drawn on both sides of the paper. So, this Möbius strip represents a two dimensional object–that is to say, you have just shown that the strip has only one side, so it must have only length and width! A Flatlander living on this strip and following the line you just drew would be unaware that the strip was rotating though the third dimension to achieve its trick: from their perspective they would be merely moving along a straight line which eventually meets up with itself, much the same as the equator eventually meets up with itself once you've traversed the circumference of the planet in our third dimension.

As we move through the fourth dimension, time, we are much like that Flatlander on the Möbius strip. To us, time feels like a straight line, moving from yesterday to today to tomorrow. But as we move along that straight line, our choices, chance, and the choices of others are constantly branching in the fifth dimension. When we look back in time, it still feels like a straight line to us, but that straight line is an illusion.

If you again imagine yourself as that fourth-dimensional creature that is a long undulating snake, how would you represent the multiple choices for action you face at every moment? Going back to our example from the second dimension, draw a letter "y" again. Now imagine this: choice and circumstance represent the place in that shape where the branch occurs, and at any moment the number of branches any one of us could take must approach an infinite number. Still, the choices at any one moment are limited by the moment before, so our representation of the fifth dimension as a "branch" is a useful convention. As you read this text, your fifth dimensional self might now have two main branches—one would be the version of you that continues reading into the next paragraph, while another would be the one who decides to take a break and go do something else. Of course, those are not the only options for what could happen in the next few seconds, so the available branches would really be much more complex than that (see Illustration 5).

THE SIXTH DIMENSION–A FOLD

As apparently boundless as the possible outcomes from one moment to the next may appear to be, there is still a much larger list of situations and events which have to fall in the "you can't get there from here" category. How would we get to the world where the 9/11/01 attacks had never occurred? How would we get to the world where human evolution had progressed differently and we all still have tails? If a time machine were possible, we could wind the clock back to whatever the precipitous events may be which those situations hinge upon, change the events, then travel forward in time again to see the new result (or, at least, one of the very many new possible results). But another much quicker path for our time machine would be like our ant marching across the newspaper: if we could fold the fifth dimension through the sixth dimension, we would be able to jump from one possible world to another without having to travel the long way back in time and forward again.

Illustration 5 – THE FIFTH DIMENSION – A SPLIT

Fig. 5-a

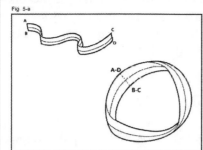

a. One of the most intriguing aspects of there being one dimension stacked on another is that down here in the dimensions below, we can be unaware of our motion in the dimensions above. Here's a simple example: if we make a Möbius strip (take a long strip of paper, add one twist to it and tape the ends together) and draw a line down the length of it, our line will eventually be on both sides of the paper before it meets back with itself. It appears, somewhat amazingly, that the strip has only one side, so it must be a representation of a two-dimensional object.

Fig. 5-b

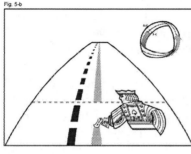

b. This means that a two-dimensional Flatlander traveling down the line we just drew would end up back where they started without ever feeling like they had left the second dimension. In reality, they would be looping and twisting in the third dimension, even though to them it felt like they were traveling in a straight line.

Fig. 5-c

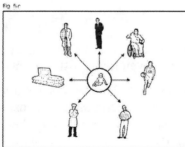

c. The fourth dimension, time, feels like a straight line to us, moving from the past to the future. But that straight line in the fourth dimension is, like the Möbius strip, actually twisting and turning in the dimension above. So, the long undulating snake that is us will feel like it is moving in a straight line in the fourth dimension, but there will actually be, in the fifth dimension, a multitude of paths that we could branch to at any given moment. Those branches will be influenced by our own choice, chance, and the actions of others.

Fig. 5-d

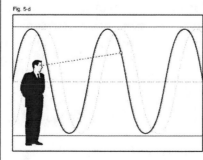

d. Quantum physics tells us that the subatomic particles that make up our world are collapsed from waves of probability simply by the act of observation. In the reality we are starting to imagine for ourselves here, we can now start to see how each of us are collapsing the indeterminate wave of probable futures contained in the fifth dimension into the fourth dimensional line that we are experiencing as "time".

One – A Quick Tour of Ten Dimensions

So, the mental shorthand would be this: the third dimension is what we move through to jump from one second-dimensional point to another. Likewise, the sixth dimension would be what we move through to jump from one fifth-dimensional point to another (see Illustration 6).

THE SEVENTH DIMENSION–A LINE

Let's stop and review for a moment. A point can be used to define a location in any dimension. So, on a two dimensional graph a point can be at the position "x, y"; while on a three dimensional graph it can be at "x, y, z", and so on. No matter what the number of dimensions, we can establish an imaginary "point" within that system by assigning a value to a co-ordinate for each dimension. For example, in four dimensions, a point could be described as being "at the corner of Scarth Street and Eleventh Avenue on the third floor, 3 o'clock this afternoon". Here we have given four co-ordinates to establish a point in the fourth dimension: three of the co-ordinates define the location in space, while the fourth co-ordinate defines the location of the point in time. Although it's impossible for us to visualize, this means a point in seven dimensions could be positioned at the location "t,u,v,w,x,y,z" on a seventh-dimensional graph.

As we keep coming back to, the first dimension is a straight line joining any two "points". One unique thing to consider now is that those two points can be very near each other or right on top of each other, so it's also easy for us to think of the first dimension as a point only. Likewise, the fourth dimension is a line joining two points in time, but it can just as easily be used to describe a specific moment in time, so we can also sometimes find ourselves imagining the fourth dimension as a point rather than a line. Now we get to the seventh dimension.

Interestingly, the number seven appears in a number of our world's spiritual systems and mystical writings as the representation of infinity/eternity, or heaven, or the highest level of spiritual awakening. How does that happen to correspond to the system we're developing here?

Illustration 6 – THE SIXTH DIMENSION – A FOLD

Fig. 6-a

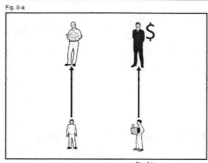

a. What if you wanted to go back into your own childhood and visit yourself? We can imagine folding the fourth dimension through the fifth, jumping back through time and space to get there. But what if you wanted to get to the world where, for example, you had created a great invention as a child that by now had made you famous and rich?

Fig. 6-b

b. We can imagine our fourth-dimensional selves branching out from our current moment into the fifth dimension, but no matter where you go from here the "great child inventor" timeline is not one of the available options in your current version of time -- "you can't get there from here" -- no matter how much choice, chance, and the actions of others become involved.

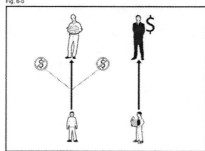

Fig. 6-c

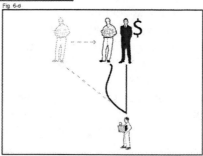

c. There are only two ways you could get to that world – one would be to travel back in time, somehow trigger the key events that caused you to come up with your invention, then travel forward in the fifth dimension to see one of the possible new worlds that might have resulted. But that would be taking the long way.

Fig 6-d

d. The shortcut we could take would involve us folding the fifth dimension through the sixth dimension, which allows us to instantly jump from our current position to a different fifth dimensional line.

The seventh dimension joins all of the possible universes our big bang could have generated to all of the possible outcomes at the other end, and treats the entire package as a single point. What will happen at the end of the universe? Some theorists have imagined a "Big Crunch", which would be somewhat like the big bang running in reverse, and many have predicted a "cold death" where entropy finally prevails. There could be many other fates we can imagine for our universe as well, some of which could be the result of unlikely coincidences, and some of which could be the result of the actions of some unimaginably advanced civilization (either human or alien) in the far distant future.

What makes the seventh dimension different is we now take the concept of *all* of the possible beginnings and their links to *all* of the possible conclusions for our particular big bang universe, and view this all simultaneously, as if it were a single point (see Illustration 7). So, for our universe, we could indeed say that a point in the seventh dimension represents infinity.[ii]   .

THE EIGHTH DIMENSION–A SPLIT

It would be easy to argue that we must be done by now. What could possibly be the next split from what we commonly know as infinity?

First of all, we should back up a moment and look at the seventh dimension a little more closely. We described the infinity of possible timelines for our universe as being a point in the seventh dimension. But that would only be part of the story, because we should then be imagining another point in the seventh dimension and drawing a line to that point to complete our description of that dimension. What would that second point be, then? It would be the multiplicity of timelines that, when perceived as a whole, represent some other completely different universe that would have been generated by some other set of initial conditions.

Illustration 7 – THE SEVENTH DIMENSION – A LINE

Fig 7-a

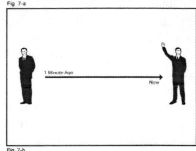

a. In our description of the fourth dimension, we imagined taking the dimension below and conceiving of it as if it were a single point. The fourth dimension is a line which can join the universe as it was one minute ago to the universe as it is right now.

Fig. 7-b

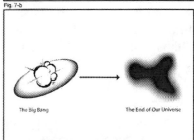

The Big Bang   The End of Our Universe

b. Or in the biggest picture possible, we could say that the fourth dimension is a line which joins the big bang to one of the possible endings of our universe.

Fig. 7-c

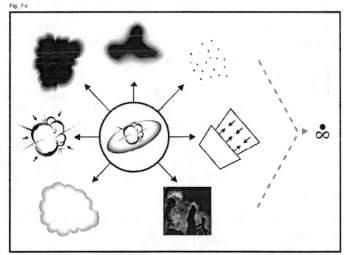

c. Now, as we enter the seventh dimension, we are about to imagine a line which treats the entire sixth dimension as if it were a single point. To do that, we have to imagine all of the possible timelines which could have started from our big bang joined to all of the possible endings for our universe (a concept which we often refer to as infinity), and treat them all as a single point. So, for us, a point in the seventh dimension would be infinity – all possible timelines which could have or will have occurred from our big bang.

One of the interesting concepts from modern physics is known as the "anthropic principle". We exist in what seems to be an impossibly complex universe where an astounding number of forces and events have aligned to create the extremely unlikely event of intelligent life as we know it today. For instance, if the force of gravity had been slightly different at the beginning, the result would have been a universe that quickly flew apart and never created stars, or a universe that immediately collapsed back in upon itself. Physicists tell us that if the constants that define our universe had varied outside of surprisingly small ranges the results, to our way of thinking, would have been catastrophic. Even within those ranges, the result could easily have been a universe that was similar to ours but still made up of a combination of elements or physical structures which did not readily support life as we know it.

According to one of the interpretations of the anthropic principle, the reason that we live in such an impossible and unlikely universe is that if all those conditions necessary to the creation of life hadn't happened to occur from the big bang onwards, then the universe wouldn't support life and we wouldn't be here to ask the question. But the interpretation of the anthropic principle that we're most interested in here tells us that all of those other universes do actually exist. Most would be completely different in ways that we can only begin to imagine, and many would (unfortunately) be unstable, short-lived or boringly uneventful. In fact, most would have physical conditions which would immediately cause a human being to cease to function.

This, then, would be a way for us to imagine the additional dimensions that will get us to the tenth. If a point in the seventh dimension represents all the possible past and future versions of the universe we live in, as generated by the very specific conditions of the very specific big bang that started our universe, then a line in the seventh dimension could be drawn to a point representing some other infinity that results from some other big bang. That line could be drawn to absolutely any other unrelated universe, or it could be one that is closely related to our own. We can imagine that travelling along that line, then, might show us a chaotic collection of seemingly unrelated infinities, or it might be an exploration (for instance) of the infinities that would have resulted from varying one specific parameter, such as the force of gravity. Still, no matter where we were on that seventh dimensional line, there would also be branches splitting off from that line that we could explore, and as soon as we choose to consider one of those alternate lines we are entering the eighth dimension (see Illustration 8).

THE NINTH DIMENSION–A FOLD

Now we're back to our ant walking across the newspaper. How would you instantaneously jump from one line exploring these different big bang universes to another completely different line? You would fold the eighth dimension through the ninth dimension. To an observer on one eighth-dimensional line of infinites resulting from a particular range of big bang conditions, you would suddenly pop out of existence. To another observer in some other completely different range of infinities associated with a separate line of big bang universes, you would suddenly appear as if by magic.

By now we are imagining a seemingly infinite number of infinities! The same dizzying order of magnitude jumps that we go through as we try to imagine the size of the solar system, to the size of a galaxy, to the size of the universe, have been compounded again and again as we rise up through the dimensions.

And in much the same way as it is impossible for us to simultaneously imagine the scale of an atom as we imagine the scale of the solar system, the only way the mind can grasp the immensity of what we are building here is to imagine it one layer at a time (see Illustration 9).

Illustration 8 - THE EIGHTH DIMENSION - A SPLIT

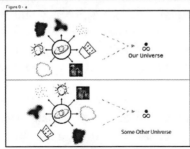

Figure 0 - a

a. When we describe infinity as being a "point" in the seventh dimension, we are only imagining part of the picture. If we're drawing a seventh dimensional line, we need to be able to imagine what a different "point" in the seventh dimension is going to be, because that's what our line is going to be joined to. But how can there be anything more than infinity? The answer is, there can be other completely different infinities created by initial conditions which are different from our own big bang.

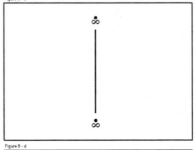

Figure 6 - b

b. Different initial conditions will create different universes where basic physical laws such as gravity and the speed of light are not the same as ours, and the resulting branching time-lines from that universe's beginning to all of its possible endings will create an infinity which is completely separate from the one which is associated with our own universe.

c. So the line we draw in the seventh dimension will join one of these infinities to another.

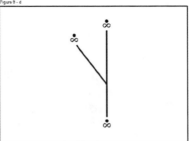

d. And, as boggling as the magnitude of what we are exploring here might be, if we were to branch off from that seventh dimensional line to draw a line to yet another infinity, we would then be entering the eighth dimension.

Illustration 9 – THE NINTH DIMENSION – A FOLD

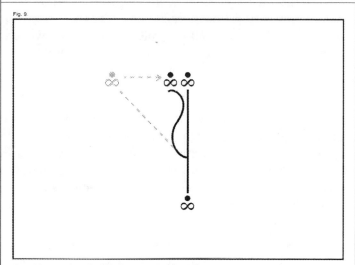

Fig. 9

As we've explored already, we can jump from one point in any dimension to another simply by folding it through the dimension above. If our ant on the newspaper were a two-dimensional Flatlander, then folding his two-dimensional world through the third dimension would allow him to magically disappear from one location and appear in a different one. As we're now imagining the ninth dimension, the same rules would apply – if we were to be able to instantaneously jump from one eighth dimensional line to another, it would be because we were able to fold through the ninth dimension.

THE TENTH DIMENSION–A POINT?

And so, finally, we arrive at the tenth dimension. Following our analogy, the tenth dimension should start by treating as a point every possible beginning and end of all the possible universes generated by all the possible big bangs (or, if you prefer, "initial conditions", since it's also possible to imagine universes which were not created by a big bang). But this time we've run out of places to go. There can be no eleventh or twelfth dimension, because we've no place left to branch or fold to: we're out of options. Effectively, what has happened to us is our beginning and end point of any lines that we attempt to draw in this dimension have become so all-inclusive that the two points are always right on top of each other, and our line is effectively the same as that dimensionless point we first imagined. As we had set out to do, it is now more easy for us to imagine the tenth dimension as the uncut fabric from which is constructed all possible universes, all possible beginnings and endings, all possible branches within all possible timelines, but without the nuances added by the geometries of the dimensions below.

Let's get back to where we started now, which is the ten spatial dimensions referred to by string theory. According to the view we've constructed here, any action or decision in the tenth dimension immediately collapses us into the dimensions below, which seems to contradict the string theory image of vibrations in the tenth dimension.

But consider this: if strings vibrating in the tenth dimension create the physical reality we experience in the dimensions below, when there is no vibration of those strings, is there nothingness in the dimensions below? From that perspective, the tenth dimension as described in these pages starts to feel like more of a fit (see Illustration 10).

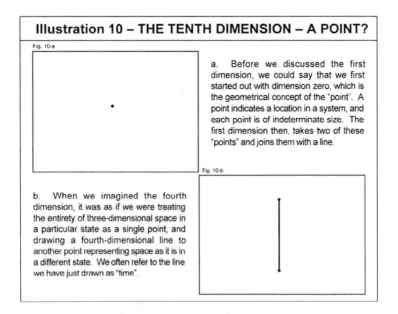

Illustration 10 – THE TENTH DIMENSION – A POINT?

Fig. 10-a

a.   Before we discussed the first dimension, we could say that we first started out with dimension zero, which is the geometrical concept of the "point". A point indicates a location in a system, and each point is of indeterminate size. The first dimension then, takes two of these "points" and joins them with a line.

Fig. 10-b

b.   When we imagined the fourth dimension, it was as if we were treating the entirety of three-dimensional space in a particular state as a single point, and drawing a fourth-dimensional line to another point representing space as it is in a different state. We often refer to the line we have just drawn as "time".

Fig. 10-c

Illustration 10 - continued

c. Then in the seventh dimension, we treated all of the possible timelines which could be generated from our big bang as if this were a single point, and imagined drawing a line to a point representing all of the possible timelines for a completely different universe.

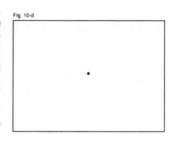

d. Now, as we enter the tenth dimension, we have to imagine all of the branches for all the possible timelines for all the possible universes and treat that as a single point in the tenth dimension. So far, so good. But this is where we hit a roadblock: if we're going to imagine the tenth dimension as continuing the cycle, and being a line, then we're going to have to imagine a different point that we can draw that line to. But there's no place left to go! By the time we have imagined all possible timelines for all possible universes as being a single point in the tenth dimension, it appears that our journey is done.

Fig. 10-d

In String theory, physicists tell us that Superstrings vibrating in the tenth dimension are what create the subatomic particles which make up our universe, and all of the other possible universes as well. In other words, all possibilities are contained within the tenth dimension, which would appear to be the concept we have just built for ourselves as we imagined the ten dimensions, built one upon another.

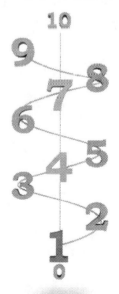

. 10
9
8
7
6
5
4
3
2
1
. 0

In the picture we've constructed here, the tenth dimension when viewed by itself becomes quite uninteresting compared to the multitude of possibilities that are generated when we descend down to the dimensions below. Speaking poetically, the tenth dimension is like white noise, an endless field of all colours and vibrations blurred together. Because it encompasses all possible realities without delineation between those realities, it is like a void. Where things do get interesting is when we cut cross-sections out of that formlessness to view some specific aspect: like our two-dimensional Flatlander viewing the feet of a human creature visiting from the dimension above as ten circles that become two, there is no way for anyone in a dimension less than ten to perceive all of the possibilities that the tenth dimension contains.

In any dimension lower than ten, all that can be viewed of reality is cross sections. But that is what makes our existence so interesting: not the infinite "white noise" of possibilities; but that out of all those possibilities that could be, we are in this very specific one, right here, and right now.

TWO–THE QUANTUM OBSERVER

According to quantum physics, particles are not particles at the subatomic level. Instead, they are waves of probabilities. The part of this theory that takes some getting used to is it has been demonstrated that it is the act of observing those probability waves which collapses them into one specific state. To be clear from the outset, there are opposing viewpoints questioning whether or not this subatomic phenomenon can be in any way translated into the physical reality that we see around us, and there is continual discussion as to where the dividing line between quantum and classical reality should be drawn.

The ongoing argument goes like this: if subatomic particles are collapsed out of their indeterminate wave function only when we observe them, doesn't it follow that we as observers are therefore creating our physical reality through the act of observation? After all, it is those subatomic particles that create the atoms and molecules of our universe.

For someone considering this line of reasoning there are questions that might immediately spring to mind. If our reality is created by the act of observation, what happened before there was an observer? Did the potential for all those other possible realities exist simultaneously, with the wave function of those particles never being collapsed? Or has there always been something that we would call an "observer", right from the beginning microseconds of our big bang, collapsing the probability wave function into the subatomic particles which eventually formed the atoms and molecules that became what we see around us now?

The opposing viewpoint has been well established for decades: quantum effects have no bearing on our physical reality, they are only significant at the subatomic level.

Quite frankly, this becomes very similar to the issues of spirituality and faith–what do you choose to believe? Either viewpoint has its proponents, and much has been written supporting both sides. In this text we are going to drop the discussion and stake out our claim: the observer, simply through the act of observing, creates reality at the subatomic level. The subatomic particles collapsed out by observation form the atoms and molecules that make up our universe. Therefore the observer is creating the physical world we see around us as well. This means that each of us is an observer, and each of us is creating our own unique reality.

This also means, according to Everett's Many Worlds theory (as briefly described in the Introduction), that all of those realities exist simultaneously but completely separate from each other. The big question that must be asked is this: if all those other realities exist, then why can't we see them?

Here is a possible explanation for this quandary that modern physicists have proposed: the other potential states that are held within quantum indeterminacy are cancelled out through a process called "decoherence". The concept of decoherence tells us that the "blurriness" of quantum indeterminacy is like the blurriness of a slightly-out-of-focus photograph: if we look very closely the blurriness is readily apparent, but the further we hold that picture away from our eyes the sharper the picture appears to be. Likewise, as we back our viewpoint out from the tiny subatomic level, and take it up to the macro-scale physical world that we live in, the other possible states implied by quantum indeterminacy become invisible to us. All of the other possible states become decoherent with the one that we are currently observing, which is why we can only see one state at a time.

In fact, "decoherence" and "many worlds" are now being used in conjunction with each other by some physicists as an explanation of how the universe functions: through the process of observation, one of the possible states for reality is made "decoherent" with the other possible realities, separating out one world from all the others and presenting us with the universe we are witness to. There are many physicists who are not willing to buy that quantum effects are relevant to our physical world. But some of those skeptics may still be able to accept the notion that we live in a unique universe which is derived from the quantum wave of all those possible other universes ("many worlds").

Incidentally, Everett's theory also states that we don't actually "collapse" the probability function, we merely observe the wave of potential in one particular state out of the many which continue to exist in the other "many worlds". In the context of our discussion this distinction is a small one, so we will continue to refer to this quantum process as "collapsing" the wave.

Most of us can readily agree that this position has the potential for many contradictions, and some will accuse this text of veering into empty-headed wishful thinking: we will make an effort in these pages to deal with those issues. For the moment, let's speak not in terms of each of us being an observer, but rather with the more dispassionate term, "the observer".

The observer, through the act of observation collapses reality from the quantum waves of probability. But this means, then, that there would be no physical reality until the observer directs their attention at some aspect of the universe. To agree to that, we also have to agree that there must be some place along the timeline stretching back to the beginning of creation where an observer came into existence. One obvious point for an observer to begin observing our known universe would be at the big bang, but with the picture we are now constructing we can start to imagine how the illusion of time that we experience as being a linear event may be clouding our judgement here. No matter where you enter from the tenth dimension, by the time you get to something resembling our version of the fourth dimension and our current space-time you will have already collapsed out a specific historic set of events which will appear to have gone back to our big bang. This is a challenging concept, so let's say it again.

Let's assume that the observer was not present at the big bang, and so the universe existed for a certain amount of time in a state of quantum indeterminacy. For the observer to have then collapsed out a reality of the complexity we see around us, the observer chooses a certain "state of being" from a long list of all aspects of physical reality, all of which are contained as potential within the tenth dimension. By choosing a very specific set of current conditions, we then must imagine that the observer has also automatically collapsed a history out of the fourth dimension that leads logically from the beginning of time to the version of reality that they are now experiencing. So, thinking in terms of the ten dimensions as we described them in the last chapter, we could say that the observer's point of entry in the tenth dimension selects one of the possible seventh dimensional universes, and from that the observer selects one of the possible fourth dimensional timelines. Looking at it in reverse order, the current space-time we are in and agree upon as being "reality" is our version of the fourth dimension, our "reality" is specifically selected from a list of other physically incompatible different-initial-conditions universes at the seventh dimension, and all of those physically incompatible universes exist simultaneously at the tenth dimension (or rather, the potential for all those universes to exist is held within the tenth dimension). Admittedly, that's a lot to digest.

What we're saying, then, is where you actually began to observe becomes irrelevant. If it tickled your fancy, you could place that first observer at, for example, 6000 years ago. To do so would mean that prior to that time all potential physical realities remained possible within the wave function, and that at that point the observer turned their attention upon our universe and collapsed the quantum wave function into the reality we see around us, complete with the impression that time had actually extended out for billions of years prior to that. But why stop there? It could also be possible then that the universe didn't actually exist until one second ago, which is when the observer turned their attention upon our universe and collapsed the probability wave function into what we now perceive as our reality, complete with a history which each of us believes we remember. Whether the observer came into existence 13.7 billion years ago or one second ago, the result will be the same: out of all the possible timelines which could have existed prior to this moment, through the act of observation we are now experiencing one of them as our own present, and our own history.

The reader may notice here that it would be very easy to substitute "God" or "The Creator" in place of "the observer" in the above paragraphs. In fact, if the reader is comfortable with the concept of each of us being an expression of God, "created in His/Her image", each with a holy spark within, then the two viewpoints are quite compatible.[iii] On the other hand though, the image of a God who is separate from, standing in judgement of, and meting out punishment to us all is much less compatible. What we are describing here is a reality where each of us is creating an expression of a specific aspect inferred within the "white noise" of the tenth dimension through our individual roles as quantum observers. If the reader finds it easier to accept the phrase "I am an aspect of God" than they do the previous sentence, then they should feel free to use that as their jumping off point instead. As we discussed before, the tenth dimension as we are conceptualizing it here is really the boring part of our discussion, because it simultaneously contains all possibilities. If we choose to imagine a Creator-God who is manifesting Himself/Herself through each one of us, we are imagining an observer who is cutting cross-sections out of the tenth dimension to examine the much more interesting and highly detailed subsets of reality which are contained within the dimensions below.

Generally, when quantum physicists talk about an observer collapsing reality, there has been a tendency in people's minds to assume that we are talking about a person. But if that were the case we would appear, with the line of reasoning we're pursuing, to be locking ourselves into a version of reality where before there were no people there was no collapsing of the quantum wave, and no physical reality. What happens if we extend our definition of possible observers to include other forms of life? Even to imagine that the first observer might have been the first primitive life-form places us in a paradox which some will not be comfortable with: the idea of a timeline instanta-neously constructed back to the big bang from wherever the first observer turned their attention on our universe is admittedly a difficult concept to accept.

However, as we will explore more in chapter five, there are many more "viewpoints" we can imagine which might be capable of collapsing the indeterminate quantum waves of probability into physical reality, and some of those could indeed exist right back to the big bang. This would also include the other physically incompatible universes which we think of as not being able support life as we know it, and could allow us to imagine completely other expressions of energy and the "desire to continue" which would result in unfathomably different lifeforms from the ones we are familiar with.

Physicists sometimes use the term "world-line"[3] to talk about the history of a particle or an object. As we discussed

---

[3] Or alternatively, "worldline", or even just "world line" – all appear to be in use.

in chapter one, time can be imagined as the line that is drawn when you take the universe as it is at one specific moment, treat that as if it were a single point, then draw a line to another point representing the universe as it is in a different state. The world-line that got us from the big bang to this current moment in time is a very specific line in the fourth dimension.

Throughout this text we will often use the word "timeline". Within the concepts we are discussing here, whether you call it a world-line or a timeline it is still referring to the same thing: it is the line you draw in time, twisting and turning as it chooses different branches in the fifth dimension, but perceived from the fourth dimension as apparently being a straight line.

Each of us has our own special viewpoint, our own unique timeline, something that separates each of us out from everyone else. Looking at the world from the perspective of each of us being a quantum observer, that uniqueness becomes unimaginably magnified: out of all the possible timelines which could have existed prior to this moment, through the act of observation each of us are now experiencing one of them as our own personal history. We'll discuss the fantastic implications of this point of view more in chapter six, "The Anthropic Viewpoint".

THREE-THE FLOW OF TIME

In 1928 the prominent British astrophysicist Sir Arthur Eddington coined the useful phrase "the arrow of time". In our day-to-day experience there is no question that time does indeed feel like an arrow, flying straight and true towards its target (the future) but never flying back towards the bow which launched it into flight.

Interestingly, though, in physics the concept of "time-reversal symmetry" shows that almost all processes and functions make just as much sense when viewed in reverse order, as if time were flying backwards. The equations of Einstein's theory of relativity work just as well whether the arrow of time flies one way or the other. So, why does our experience of time appear to flow only in one direction? I would suggest that it's because we're complex organisms evolved from processes moving in that direction.

All basic chemical processes have an equal logic viewed in reverse order, even the ones that from our point of view appear to be only possible to move in one direction. If we have a specific chemical reaction which we'll call "A plus B always equals C", then in a world where time flows in the reverse direction C minus B would always equal A, regardless of whether C minus B is a reaction that can occur within our current perception of the universe. It would be easy to argue that this discussion is pointless: since time doesn't flow in the reverse direction, the reverse chemical process of C minus B can never occur. But what if it is our perception as a quantum observer that makes us believe that time flows only in one direction?

In that primordial soup where the first chemical processes that became the spark of life were forming, let's try to imagine now that it is purely coincidence that those processes happened to be moving in the direction that we now perceive as "forward" in time: that is to say, that we just happened to develop from some of the thermodynamic "A plus B equals C" processes rather than the "C minus B equals A" processes. Could a completely different form of life spring from those reverse order reactions? Could there have been competing processes back then which attempted to organize themselves in the reverse direction, trying to become life on a timeline which moved from what we now perceive of as the present to the past?

And what about at the other end of the long timeline which represents the lifespan of our universe? Clearly, there are a great many timelines (or "world-lines") which could potentially be drawn to represent our universe's potential beginnings-to-endings. For instance, if the universe ends in a "Big Crunch" (which we referred to in chapter one) this is easier to imagine, because a Big Crunch could have processes within it which, when viewed in reverse order could be somewhat similar to the big bang conditions from which life eventually began for us. But even a "cold death"– another of the possible futures for our universe, where entropy finally prevails–viewed on a reverse timeline would appear to be a gradual organization of matter that could also be a springboard for the processes of another form of life: a form of life that would be collapsing reality in the reverse direction to ours.

Three – The Flow of Time

The Steven Strogatz book "Sync" describes many instances where order seems to spontaneously spring from disorder in the universe, and in nature. Some of the processes this groundbreaking book touches upon could conceivably result in life forming on the reverse-timeline coming back from a cold death universe.

As unlikely as it is to occur, let's consider what a meeting of two lifeforms moving in opposite directions on their fourth dimensional timeline would be like. First of all, for these two lifeforms the actions of cause and effect would be completely inexplicable to each other. Communication would be virtually impossible. Actions of the opposing group would appear to be random, or without a discernible motivation.

Let's imagine that an alien race arrives on the planet Earth in the year 3000 and finds it uninhabited. Their timeline is moving in the opposite direction to ours. They decide they really like the planet, and gradually increase their population, until by our year 2500 they have entirely taken it over. But then, an inexplicable race that calls themselves "human beings" slowly starts appearing, and over the next few centuries this new race becomes increasingly dominant, killing off the alien invaders one by one, until by the year 2000 the aliens are vanquished forever. Humanity wins! Or does it?

Humanity's version of the same events, of course, would be the opposite. In the year 2000 there would be a few isolated and largely unreported incidents where a smattering of human beings meet up with hostile but disorganized alien creatures and kill them. By 2100, the aliens would be much more of a threat, a threat which gradually becomes unstoppable, and by the year 2500 no more humans would remain. The aliens win! Or do they?

The question "or do they?" is not as flippant as it might seem. It should be clear that in the scenario above both races were vanquished according to their own timeline, resulting in each other's mutual destruction. Humanity is wiped out by five hundred years from now in our future, and the reverse-time aliens are (from their perception) wiped out one thousand years after arriving here on the planet. Is it possible to imagine a scenario where both races win? Here's one that gets to the root of the discussion of cause and effect and how it relates to our experience of the fourth dimension.

Let's suppose that those reverse-time aliens arrived on earth five minute ago, bent on killing us all and taking over the planet. According to humanity's current timeline, we have no record and no knowledge of those aliens arriving then. Therefore, our future continues to move forward, unaffected by their actions. On our own timeline we can look back and see a long history of humanity stretching back through the generations, whose life was in no way affected by the presence of these destructive invaders. (Humanity wins! Or does it?) And yet, we can also imagine the aliens are successful in their takeover, and that as they move back into our history they wipe us all out. But how can the aliens win in what we think of as our past, and yet we could continue to have long happy lives in our own present and future? This relates to the famous paradoxes of time travel, a subject which we will devote an entire chapter to later in this book.

Admittedly, the idea of a creature whose sense of time moves in the opposite direction to ours is a difficult concept to fathom. Think of this as a mental game that helps us to free our minds, allowing us to imagine how time is more than just a mysterious one-way arrow that we superimpose over our physical reality. After all, in the first dimension there is no such "one-way" restriction–we can freely imagine a line that joins point A to point B just as easily as we can imagine moving along the same line to get from point B to point A. With powerful enough technology or the properly equipped viewpoint of a quantum observer, the limitation we feel of time moving only in one direction should eventually come to be seen as a uniquely limited viewpoint that is not really relevant to the actual structure of the fourth dimension and above.

Let's look at one of the more difficult scientific concepts to get used to because it appears to violate our own "common sense" knowledge of how the world works. Here's what we know from our own experience: if you're on the highway going 99, and someone passes you going 100, then from your perspective it would be the same as if you were motionless and the person passed you at a speed of 1. But the speed of light, as a constant, is completely independent of our activities down here in space-time. This means even when we're on some inconceivably technologically advanced spaceship capable of moving at close to the speed of light, we can never "catch up" to light. In fact, as hard as this might be to imagine, if we were travelling at 99% of the speed of light, a beam of light that we were chasing would still seem to be moving away from us at 100% of the speed of light.

In the ten dimensions as we're imagining them, the speed of light is defined by interactions in a higher dimension than the one we live in. This is how it can be independent of how we move in the fourth dimension, time. As we learned from Einstein's special theory of relativity, when we approach the speed of light, time appears to "stretch", so for the occupants of the spaceship time is slowing down, while to an outside observer the occupants are travelling in time much faster.

This is a hard idea for us to accept, but once we do we can use it as a way to imagine how time travel in the opposite direction is possible for our reverse-time beings. Here's what we're trying to get to: the speed of light, as an "independent constant", is unaffected by whatever speed we as observers of the speed of light are travelling. What we're proposing now is that this concept applies not only to the speed but the direction we are moving in time. So a creature whose point of view is moving in the opposite direction in time to ours would be collapsing quantum waves of probability in the opposite direction as well, and would still see that no matter how fast they travelled, the speed of light would continue to zip away from them at exactly the same value. The time-reversal symmetry of Einstein's special theory of relativity tells us they would be able to use near-speed-of-light travel as a form of time travel just like us, but in the opposite direction–for them it would be a way to more quickly get to our past.

The concept of being able to travel to the past is not just from the realm of science fiction. Many theoretical physicists have come up with scenarios where this could be scientifically possible. For instance, Scottish physicist W. J. van Stockum proposed in 1937 that a very dense and infinitely long cylinder spinning about its infinitely long axis would, according to the laws of general relativity, set up a whirlpool-like vortex in space and time which would cause spaceships circling the cylinder to travel backwards in time. Kurt Gödel proposed in 1949 that if the entire universe were rotating (a situation which would be difficult or impossible for us to be aware of because there would be no stationary object "outside the universe" for us to judge our rotation against), there would be trajectories a spaceship could follow which would move it back to the time before it set out. "Wormholes" in the fabric of space, though familiar enough to science fiction fans, have actually been explored as a concept by serious theoretical physicists such as Kip Thorne and Stephen Hawking, who proposed that some day in the distant future these could prove to offer a pathway to other times or physical points within the universe.

At present, it appears the largest obstacle that will stand in the way of developing a workable time travel technology may not be whether it's theoretically possible, but that such massive amounts of energy will be required to achieve success. For the time being, then, using a wormhole to jump to the moon or the day before yesterday is still just science fiction. In the chapter "The Paradoxes of Time Travel", we'll discuss the different kinds of wormholes that there could possibly be according to the theory we're exploring now.

Could it be that there are other processes in our current reality that are actually moving in the opposite direction along the "line of time", and that is why they are so hard to predict? What if there was a cause and effect that was rippling back towards us from some future event? From our limited viewpoint, not knowing what the original event is going to be would make the results we experience now seem mysterious and unpredictable. But this is not to say that we couldn't use the same forensic science abilities we have developed for detecting other events which are invisible or unavailable to us to eventually determine what that future event is going to be. Let's explore a completely fanciful example.

Suppose that some suitably long time in the future the earth is going to be destroyed by a gigantic meteor impact. What if that impact were to have created a resonance in the structure of the earth that rippled backwards in time? Like a recording of a cymbal crash played in reverse, there would be comparatively weak vibrations for a long time, which would then begin to grow somewhat as we approached the impact, till in the final moments or seconds before impact the vibration would grow exponentially. Now, what if we were to suppose that those reverse-moving ripples were a part of what causes the tectonic shifts that influence the triggering of earthquakes? From our viewpoint, the relationship between those events would be much more obscure, because our limited vantage point makes us assume that all cause-and-effect moves in one direction only.

The instantaneous interaction of distantly separated subatomic particles is an example of an action that defies our experience of time being a line that moves in one direction. In the 1930's Einstein famously objected to implications that such interactions were even possible, dismissing them as "spooky action at a distance". A paper on this subject published by Einstein, Podolsky and Rosen in 1935 appeared to prove that quantum physics, because it appeared to allow such impossibilities, was an imperfect description of the nature of reality. Nonetheless, since the

1980's there have been numerous experiments carried out in labs around the world that have proved such instantaneous interactions at a distance can and do occur, seemingly in violation of the limit placed by Einstein's theories on the existence of any faster-than-light connections. While the researchers conducting these experiments are quick to point out that the faster-than-light limitation is really not being violated here, what they are achieving is nonetheless quite amazing.

In these experiments, physicists have been able to use a process known as "entanglement" to imbue certain defining characteristics on pairs or clusters of particles, and more recently even on clusters of atoms. When these particles are separated from each other it can then be shown that they somehow remain in "communication" with each other, so that observing the properties of one particle or cluster will instantaneously reveal the same aspect within the other. While this revelation may seem to hold the seeds of an instantaneous form of data transmission, the limitation of this seemingly miraculous connection is that there is currently no way for scientists to "select" what the result is going to be. So, while the distantly separated particles are still somehow entwined, all that can happen at present is that by collapsing the quantum wave of possibilities for one particle, scientists can then instantaneously know what the corresponding entwined particle is also going to reveal.

Entanglement is easily explained within the dimensional concepts we are now exploring. We can imagine that these atoms are still directly connected or somehow directly adjacent to each other in a higher spatial dimension, even though they may be, for example, 11 kilometres away from each other in the third dimension (as they were in the entanglement experiment conducted by Nicolas Gisin and his team at the University of Geneva in 1997). With entanglement, it seems possible that we are seeing direct evidence of actions in higher-dimensional geometry that show how time is just another spatial dimension rather than a separate concept. And from our new perspective, we have another way to show that Einstein's concepts regarding "no faster-than-light motion" are not being violated.

As we've said, the speed of light is a constant. What do we know about constants and superstrings? According to string theory, the speed of light would be related to a number of constants that are set up in our universe by specific vibrations of superstrings in the tenth dimension.

The long-held belief is that constants such as gravity or the speed of light will be the same no matter where or when we go within our universe. Actually, there is currently new research that seems to indicate that those physical constants may have subtly shifted over the eons, and that there could be distant parts of the currently visible universe where those constants are slightly different.[4] Whether that proves to be the case or not will have no bearing on our discussion here, because in either case the nature of reality will be defined by the vibration of these superstrings, and it's entirely possible that those vibrations might be slightly different at different parts of the timeline of the universe. In chapter ten, we will argue that the drift of physical constants might actually be an example of our universe travelling along a line (or branch) in the seventh (or eighth) dimension, a concept that we're not quite ready for in this part of our discussion.

As we have been careful to note, our concept of time being a full spatial dimension is often not the accepted notion within the world of physics. Interestingly, science has a bit of a split personality when it comes to discussions of time. So, while Einstein's theories (and the theories that follow from his concepts) seem to indicate that "space-time" is a tangible fabric which can be bent and stretched, there are many other examples where science treats time as being a completely separate entity: in other words, time becomes a quality which gets overlaid on top of the other spatial

---

[4] We must keep in mind here that when we are viewing an immensely distant part of our universe, we are also viewing something from a much earlier point in time of the universe's history, because of the time it took the light from that part of the universe to reach us. In other words, distance equals time, so these immense distances give us a window back to another time.

Three – The Flow of Time

dimensions, rather than being just another dimension which is woven together with the ones above and below it.

There are string theorists though, who have been expressing their reservations about the scientific tradition of treating time as a separate element from space. This has led to many interesting quotes, where string theorists are starting to express concepts which we once expected to hear only from yogis and gurus. Nathan Seiberg, of Princeton's Institute for Advanced Studies was quoted in the Los Angeles Times as saying "I am almost certain that space and time are illusions". Edward Witten (one of the most respected researchers in modern physics, and the man who first advanced M-Theory) has said that "time and space may be doomed". Viewpoints such as these hint that the way of looking at the dimensions we are exploring in this book may not be a outlandish as some might think.

Often, when theorists discuss the possibilities of moving through time as if it were a true spatial dimension, phrases like "timelike curves" and "closed timelike loops" are used to keep such discussions separate from science's traditional description of time.

We have already touched briefly on the concept of world-lines: a world-line is an example of a timelike curve in space-time. Einstein first used the term as he developed his theories of relativity, and physicists still use it to refer to the history of an object or a particle.

One commonly referenced example of a world-line is the orbit of the earth: viewed in the third dimension, the orbit is more or less a circle as it travels around the sun. A world-line graphing this motion would plot time against the X and Y position, so the orbit of the earth would look like a coil rather than a circle. By one year from now the earth will have returned to its current position in space, but it will be at a different place in time, so the world-line representing that motion will never create a closed loop: it will instead be an open-ended spiral.

A world-line representing the motion of the earth around the sun is a simple enough concept to imagine. The world-line representing the history of a person's life, or the history of the universe, is a much more complex line, but the basic concept is the same. And, to veer into even more fanciful territory for a moment, the world-line representing a person who is able to travel in time to their own past would be an example of someone travelling on a "closed timelike loop". In chapter seven, "The Paradoxes of Time Travel", we will look at a wonderful trilogy by novelist Greg Bear in which he depicts a future where we are able to explore and manipulate world-lines to visit alternate worlds that are potentially held within the higher dimensional geometries. Mr. Bear engages in lively conversations with the many readers and fans visiting his website (www.gregbear.com), where he discusses the ideas behind his works of fiction. On his website and in interviews elsewhere over the years, Mr. Bear has good-naturedly referred to some of his novels as containing his own "crackpot theories". Nonetheless, some of his novels have received extensive critical praise for their strong scientific content.

"Crackpot theories" is a concept we return to a few more times in the upcoming pages. While the idea of manipulating word-lines may seem like nothing more than a crackpot science fiction concept at this time, it is also an idea which is easily imagined and explained within the context of the ideas we are exploring in this book. Nonetheless, it may be somewhat surprising to learn that the idea of scientists stacking or braiding the world-lines of subatomic particles as a way to create "quantum computers" is now being advanced, and receiving serious coverage in magazines such as Scientific American.

Despite the conclusion one might draw from some of the popular writing on the subject, the term "String theory" does not in fact refer to a single dominant concept. Generally speaking, the five competing versions of what is usually thought of as falling under the umbrella of that term describe the ten dimensions as being constructed from six additional "compactified" dimensions above the four we live in. That is usually interpreted to mean that string theory is really based upon nine spatial dimensions, and a tenth one which is time. M-Theory, on the other hand, provides a way of unifying the five most commonly accepted (and competing) string theories by supposing that there is an eleventh dimension which at low energies gives rise to something called "supergravity", an advanced concept which is beyond our scope of discussion.

One of the concepts that has sprung from M-Theory is that our reality is actually created in ten spatial dimensions, plus an eleventh dimension which is "time".[5] With the revelation that superstrings could have been vibrating with slightly different energies at different times in the history of the universe, one might argue that we have indeed added an eleventh dimension (of time as experienced by superstrings) to our discussion. But we could then argue that there should therefore be a twelfth dimension where superstring vibra-tions are branching into different potential timelines, and a thirteenth dimension where we can jump from one of those timelines to another, and even a fourteenth dimension where we consider all of those branching timelines as if they were a single point. Quite frankly, this is not the picture of reality we were hoping to build (someone else can write the book "Imagining the Fourteenth Dimension", as it holds no fascination for me). The way out of this quandary is to

---

[5] Some modern theories use the eleventh dimension to derive the different shapes and harmonic modes of the superstrings that are vibrating in the tenth dimension. This would be a somewhat different interpretation of the eleventh dimension, but related to our discussion because it still uses a dimension higher than the tenth to imagine how the motion and shape of the strings is being derived, which in a sense is still the aspect of time as it relates to the movement of strings in the tenth dimension. Our argument remains the same – by imagining that time is one of the physical dimensions, we are imagining that the shapes and vibrations of the superstrings are derived from the dimensions below, rather than above, the tenth dimension where those strings reside. Lisa Randall's "Warped Passages" explains other new thinking about the eleventh dimension as it pertains to branes, supersymmetry breaking, supergravity and the nature of reality at low and high energy levels, but she also makes it clear that in many senses the tenth and eleventh dimension may just be two ways of looking at the same thing.

Also, it could be noted here that in 1996 Cumrun Vafa announced a Twelfth Dimensional theory of reality which is called "F-Theory" . Once again, we would have to argue here that such embellishments to String Theory requiring dimensions above the Tenth will eventually be proven to be unnecessary.

Three – The Flow of Time

remember that our personal experience of time is based upon a limited one-way-arrow viewpoint of the fourth spatial dimension.

Here's another way to think about whether our theory of reality requires there to be an eleventh dimension. When we talk about strings vibrating in the tenth dimension, what are we really imagining? Is somebody or something arranging those strings in specific configurations, and plucking them to make them vibrate? Is some unseen hand tuning these strings up and down, causing them to vibrate at higher or lower frequencies, with the higher energy vibrations being converted into subatomic particles that have greater mass? When we talk about the nodes or harmonics of a superstring vibration creating different subatomic particles, are we imagining that someone is touching these strings at their halfway point to create octave harmonics, and so on (see Illustration 11)? And if we were to actually imagine these things were happening, what dimension would the entity which is plucking those strings inhabit? The answer, once again, is contained within our concept of how the tenth dimension is different from the others below it.

As we first discussed in chapter one, the tenth dimension is intimately tied with the indeterminate nature of quantum physics, and our role as quantum observers. Through the act of observation, we are defining a particular mode of existence which is only implied within the ways that strings in the tenth dimension potentially could behave.

This may seem like a classic chicken and egg argument, but it's an important distinction. By observing a certain reality, we are collapsing out what the results of certain superstring vibrations would have been had they been vibrating, and effectively this is exactly the same thing as observing the reality that results from the vibrations of strings in the tenth dimension. We could say that nothing ever really happens in the tenth dimension, because as soon as anything "tries to", it immediately collapses out a reality in the dimensions below.

Three – The Flow of Time

Illustration 11 - HARMONICS

Fig. 11-a

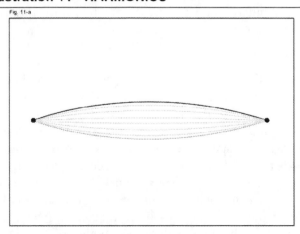

a. The concept of "harmonics" might be more familiar to anyone who has played a stringed instrument. When you pluck a string on a guitar or violin, the action is not as simple as you might imagine. While it might appear to your eye that the string is simply moving back and forth to describe a gentle curve that is widest at the middle of the string, there are other vibrational patterns that are also part of the string's motion, and the proportion of those other vibrational patterns is what gives each instrument its unique timbre.

Fig. 11-b

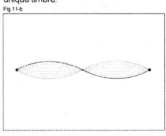

Fig. 11-c

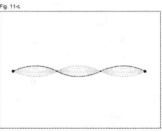

b. We can more clearly see the other competing patterns by lightly touching the string at various points along the string when we strike it, and we call these other vibration modes "harmonics" or "partials". So, by touching the string at its half way point we cause the perceived note to jump up an octave, and a high speed photograph would show us that the string is now vibrating in a pattern that describes two equal curves rather than one, with each curve occupying half the length of the string. The point we touched in the middle of the string would now appear to not be vibrating, and we can call that point a node.

c. Now, if we touch the string at the one third point we can create a note which is an octave and fifth higher, which would be the next harmonic, and our high speed photograph would show the string now vibrating with two nodes dividing the string into three equal sections. Dividing the string at the one-quarter mark produces a note two octaves up, and so on up through a series of harmonics, all of which are part of the main vibration of the open string when we pluck it.

The strings in superstring theory then, can have different vibrational modes that create different subatomic particles, in the same way that a guitar string has its main vibration but other harmonics contained within that vibration as well.

Three – The Flow of Time

In this book, "time" is always the way that we move within any dimension from one state to another, and it is always being drawn by a point (or a series of points) moving along a line in the next dimension up from the one we are currently examining. Down here in the third dimension, we think of time being the fourth dimension. If we were sixth-dimensional beings, we would think of time being the seventh dimension, and so on. In the ninth dimension, this would mean that the tenth dimension is time. But this is not to be interpreted as saying that in the version of reality we're exploring here, time is always the tenth dimension. Nor are we saying in these pages that time for the tenth dimension would be in the eleventh dimension.

We have already discussed the "split personality" that science seems to have when it comes to discussions of time. There are many opportunities for confusion because of this. For instance: if ten-dimensional string theory says that there are nine spatial dimensions plus a tenth one which is time, could we interpret that to mean that in string theory time is really the tenth dimension? Or there is M-Theory, which says there is the dimension of time, plus ten spatial dimensions. Is time the eleventh dimension in M-Theory, or in that theory is time still way down below in the fourth dimension? And even Kaluza-Klein theory, which is an important cornerstone of string theory, says that for our universe the basic laws of light and gravity are defined in four dimensions of space, plus a fifth dimension which is time. In that theory is time the fifth dimension?

The version of the ten dimensions in these pages attempts to clear up this issue by saying that time is an effect of our actions as quantum observers, and because the indeterminate wave-state exists in any and all of the dimensions, time can be thought of as being in any dimension we choose to examine. By defining our reality as having ten spatial dimensions (with the tenth one admittedly having a uniquely unchanging indeterminate status separate and above the other nine), we are proposing a way to unify any thoughts of there being nine spatial dimensions, or ten spatial dimensions, or even eleven dimensions which include a dimension of time.

If we examine the helix graphic on this book's cover (or on the companion website for this book), we see eleven numbers are represented: the numbers one through ten, plus the number zero. As we saw in chapter one, that "zero" represents not a full dimension, but rather just the geometric concept of a point: a point can be of specific location, but of indeterminate size.

We also touched on how we sometimes think of time as being a process through which change occurs, while in other cases we think of time as being a specific co-ordinate: if I am arranging to meet you at a location and time, I am defining that as a specific point in the fourth dimension. As we've already discussed, four dimensions means four variables must be defined: there are the x,y,z values that define our meeting place in the first three dimensions, plus the additional co-ordinate that defines the meeting time (for instance, "3 o'clock tomorrow afternoon"). This may sound like we have completely defined a point in four dimensions for our meeting, but there is still some opportunity for confusion over what we're really referring to here, if we are thinking of the fourth dimension as being more than just time.

Here is the problem: let's refer to that point in the fourth dimension we have set for our meeting as point "M". In the fourth dimension there are still a great many states that could occur once we arrive at point "M": we could both show up, I could be late, the world could be destroyed and we both miss the meeting. Each of those is at a version of point "M" in the fourth dimension. Each of those possible "states" is specifically observed from all the possible wave-states, and only one of those states will be the one which we as quantum observers participating in a consensual reality will find ourselves viewing tomorrow at point "M". This is where the indeterminate size of a point becomes so important to us: that point "M" for tomorrow's meeting, when we arrive there and see which outcome actually occurs, is a point that represents a very specific slice chosen from the unfathomably huge list of possible outcomes that could have been observed. Also, each of those outcomes has its own trajectory of other points that got us to that point, and a most likely set of points that will follow.

This is an extremely important part of the concept we are exploring. If we can accept that from here in the third dimension "time" is a point, or a set of discrete points, moving along a line in the dimension above, and that the indeterminate size of that point is what makes it encompass much more than just the limited location in time and space that we tend to think of it as being, then we can see a useful interpretation which says that time is "Dimension Zero" . This concept provides us with a way to imagine ten spatial dimensions, and it provides us with a way to imagine the slipperiness of the definition of time (Is time a point, as in "3 pm tomorrow"? Is time a line, as in "the meeting took an hour"? Or is time really just a series of points so close together that they feel like a continuous line?). This concept also gives us a useful way to imagine how time is the way you move from one particular state to another within the dimension below, no matter what dimension you are currently examining.

However, I have to admit I am hesitant to use the phrase "Dimension Zero" as the way to describe time, because of the inference that could then be drawn that I am claiming that dimension zero is a full dimension. If you, dear reader, find it useful to think of dimension zero as being time, then please feel free to continue to use that concept for the remainder of this book.

Clearly, for persons used to other established ways of viewing the universe, the version of reality I am proposing here may be hard to accept. The explanation of how the eleven dimensions are derived as we have just described it is not found in any textbook on string theory or being taught in any university. Where this view *is* compatible, though, is with the rapidly growing acceptance amongst cosmologists of the possibility that our universe as we know it is part of a

"multiverse": a collection of many other universes, all of
which are implied by the probability wave function of
quantum physics.

So. Is "Imagining the Tenth Dimension" a crackpot theory
from a non-physicist with no formal background in the
relevant sciences? Absolutely. I am making no claims at all
about the viability of this theory's mathematics, as I do not
have the tools to even begin such an analysis. The
suppositions we are exploring here are based purely upon
intuition, combined with a layman's understanding of the
concepts of quantum mechanics and superstrings. The fault
for any misrepresentations of string theory or the laws of
physics that may occur within these pages rests squarely on
my shoulders, and not with any of the other sources cited
throughout this text.

While the view we are exploring now may be challenging,
there are many theories of reality out there being advanced
by respected physicists which the general public may find
even harder to imagine: "Brane Cosmology", for instance, is
not a crackpot theory, it is one of the newer frontrunners in
trying to imagine the fabric of space and time. It is based
upon the concept that our universe is trapped on a three
dimensional membrane, which physicists call a "three-
brane". Parts of the strings of string theory would be
embedded in this brane. One could imagine a seventh-
dimensional brane, or "seven-brane", which our three-brane
could be interacting with, and so on.

One version of Brane Cosmology includes a concept being
advanced for the origin of the universe which has the lovely
nickname of the "Big Splat". It suggests that near our own
three-brane there could be another, in which a parallel
universe to ours is contained. Every trillion years or so, this
theory suggests, the two branes, which are ordinarily
separated from each other in the fourth spatial dimension,
are drawn together and eventually smash into each other,
creating two brand new universes with resulting processes
that would then appear from within our brane-universe to be

very similar to the big bang. We'll discuss the Big Splat theory more in the chapter "Dark Matter and Other Mysteries".

Amazing theories such as the Big Splat beg the question, how do you prove it? New high energy particle accelerators (which may reveal some of the basic subatomic particles that have been predicted by some of the recent scientific theories, but which are as yet undetected), and ultra-sensitive measuring devices (which may show the existence of "gravity waves", a predicted outcome from some of the current theories of the origin of the universe) are coming on line each year which provide cosmologists with new tools that might allow them to see hints of the structures implied within these theories. But there are still a great many mysteries to be solved.[6]

One of the great mysteries of the universe was first proposed in 1823 by Heinrich Wilhelm Olbers. "Olber's Paradox" asks this deceptively simple question–if the universe is infinite, then why is the night sky mostly black? No matter what direction you look in the night sky, there should be an infinitude of stars. While it's true that the further away a star is, the dimmer its light will be, it is also true that with an infinite universe, the further away you look in any specific direction the more stars there should be, so the amount of light from any direction will continue to combine. It can be shown that these two factors, the dimming over distance and the summing of light from additional stars, should exactly cancel each other out. Therefore the night sky should be white, not black.

---

[6] As an aside, the reader may notice there are places in this text that we are using the terms "cosmologist" and "physicist" somewhat interchangeably. A cosmologist is a physicist who is looking at the big picture of the universe, trying to discover and describe the underlying organizing principles that make it work. In the twentieth century there was much about the field of cosmology that was purely speculative. But with the most recent advances in research (for instance the "Wilkinson anisotropy probe", or WMAP satellite as it is more commonly known, which beginning in February 2003 has been giving us images of our universe from back when it was just a baby, only 380,000 years old) cosmologists have much more hard data to work with now.

Three – The Flow of Time

The first person to answer this paradox, interestingly enough, was the American fiction author Edgar Allan Poe. In 1848, just a year before his death at the age of forty, he completed an essay of his observations and suppositions in a rambling work called "Eureka: A Prose Poem". Poe, who considered the work to be his career masterpiece, wanted it to be considered as art rather than science. Nonetheless, within its pages he anticipated the big bang theory by eighty years, and solved Olber's paradox over fifty years before a scientific proof was to be developed (by Lord Kelvin in 1901). Poe proposed that the night sky is black because of the immense distances to the outermost reaches of the universe, which means that the light from those most distant stars has not reached us yet. It turns out that is indeed the correct answer—our universe is not infinitely old, because if it were then our night sky would be white, not black.

And it is our unique experience as quantum observers who are collapsing the "arrow of time" out of the fourth dimension in the particular direction that we are right now (with the big bang appearing to launch the arrow and the future as the arrow's undetermined target) which provides us with that beautiful vision of a black sky and a host of twinkling stars.

FOUR-THE BINARY VIEWPOINT

It has been suggested that it is a male viewpoint to want to categorize everything, and a female viewpoint to want to view things holistically. This is not to say that one approach is better than the other, but rather to point out that there are usually many ways we can analyze the same information.

The binary viewpoint, where everything can be summed up by simply categorizing any item as "here are the things it is" and "here are the things it isn't" would, one might say, be a male viewpoint taken to the extreme. But if we follow that reasoning, we can think of the tenth dimension as the ultimate shopping list of yes and no answers for every possible aspect of reality. We are all moving within a tiny aspect contained within the tenth dimension, each moment we experience being the result of a seemingly infinite number of yes/no answers made back to the beginning of time.

If we can agree that our conception of time as a one-way "arrow" is an illusion created by our unique point of view, then ultimately we can come to the viewpoint that the big bang is also an illusion, as it is just a side effect of collapsing the tenth dimension with the very first yes/no. The point at which we enter the tenth dimensional system becomes the big bang (that is to say, the beginning) for the dimensions below. The currently accepted version of the big bang is known as "inflationary cosmology", in which it is proposed that the size of the universe increased by a factor greater than a million trillion trillion in less than a millionth of a trillionth of a trillionth of a second. Does this mind-boggling amount of sudden inflation not sound more like the flipping of a gigantic yes/no toggle switch?

To be clear, this is not to say that the observed effects of the big bang don't exist, or that the extraordinary expansion described in inflationary cosmology didn't happen. Rather, the point here is that there are others ways of viewing the concept of the big bang that would help us to imagine what "before the big bang" might be.[iv] What we are describing here is not an attempt to disprove the conventional viewpoint cosmologists have of the history of the universe, but rather to provide another way of looking at the same set of data. If we view the history of the big bang along a linear time line, we come up with the traditional viewpoint of that process. But if we analyze the timeline of our universe from the viewpoint of time being another spatial dimension which can be freely navigated within, we can find new ways of analyzing those same events.

The same data can often have more than one interpretation. Sometimes that's because one interpretation is right and the other is wrong: if we're presented with the image of the sun travelling through the sky above a flat horizon, we might advance the theory that the sun travels around the earth and the earth is flat. In that case, there is a different way to interpret the data (the earth travels around the sun, and the earth is so large that we can't easily see its curvature), which turns out to disprove the other theory. Or, at the very least, we can say that there is no way that we can simultaneously believe both interpretations of the data.

Four – The Binary Viewpoint

But that is not always the case. In fact, there are many examples in science where the same data has multiple interpretations and each, in its own way, may be correct. When Newton discovered the laws which allowed him to predict the orbits of planets around stars, and even the unusual elliptical orbits of comets, he gave the world a way of understanding gravity that would not be challenged for centuries. When Einstein revealed that gravity was actually a bending of space-time, did that mean that Newton's equations were proven wrong? No. Both approaches describe the same observed data, but from different viewpoints. Although Newton believed that gravity was an instantaneous force across the universe and Einstein proved this particular supposition wrong, Newton's calculations continue to successfully predict the motion of bodies as they are affected by gravity. One could say that Einstein's theories incorporated Newton's laws, acting as an additional overlay which helps to explain and clarify what Newton observed, rather than contradicting or disproving it.

One of the most satisfying experiences for scientists, it could be said, is when a new explanation or interpretation that supplants an old one is actually less complex. Einstein is quoted as saying that we should try to make things "as simple as possible, but no simpler". The underlying thought behind his statement is that the laws and structures of reality are not random collections of information, and if it sometimes appears that way, it is only because there is a deeper aspect of the structures that has yet to be revealed to us. For instance, the "Standard Model", developed in the 1970s, is often used as an example of a theory which (although useful) was a bit of a Frankenstein's Monster of stuck together parts. 19 measurement values had to be entered as arbitrary numbers because they were not derived from or predicted by the theory. Despite its inelegant structure, the Standard Model was a very successful tool for the prediction of new subatomic particles which at that point had not yet been seen. String Theory, if proven once and for all to be the correct vision of the underlying structures of reality, supplants and explains the Standard

Model with a simpler, more "elegant" theory which shows where those 19 seemingly arbitrary values actually come from.

Newer, simpler theories that enhance the understanding of older, more complex ones continue to come to light. M-Theory, the current version of string theory, actually ties together what were previously thought to be five competing versions of string theory, and shows how each are only different aspects of the bigger picture described by M-Theory. String theorists propose that gravitational effects are actually the result of the exchange of so-far undetected particles known as "gravitons", and that gravitons represent the particle that would be generated by the lowest possible "note" of a vibrating superstring. If gravitons are eventually proven to exist, would that mean that Einstein's concept of gravity being a bending of space-time has been proven to be erroneous, or that Newton's laws of motion were no longer applicable? Once again, not at all. We would merely have come up with yet another way of interpreting the same data.

Similarly, in these pages we are proposing that any process we describe as existing across linear time has other ways it can be described. By the time you view the seventh dimension, where all possible beginnings and endings for any particular universe can be contained within a single point, we start to imagine how the ways of viewing that construct are not limited to starting at the "beginning" and tracing a line to the "ending". There are many other ways of cutting a cross-section through such a fabric which are independent of our limited "one-dimensional" experience of time.

This means that there should also be ways of entering the system that are the "reverse-direction version"–which, in our case, would probably mean we are imagining a universe that very gradually coalesces from the "cold death" of entropy.

In our universe, it seems that entropy is an inexorable process moving from the past to the future, from which we can never escape. One popular notion within modern physics is that the apparently unlikely amount of order within our current universe as we are now witnessing it is not, as one might surmise, because the universe has evolved out of chaos into a more ordered state since the big bang. In fact, it would be the opposite: physicists are proposing that the universe was ordered to an even more unlikely degree by the processes of the big bang and inflationary cosmology. The somewhat surprising conclusion of this viewpoint, then, is that it is this natural process of gradual decline, from order to disorder, from high energy to low energy, that is responsible for the surprising degree of organization that our current universe possesses.

This would seem to be proof that time can only flow in one direction. However, Steven Strogatz, in his groundbreaking book "Sync", describes many instances where order seems to spontaneously spring from disorder in the universe, and in nature. While his theories of sync are, of course, based upon the observations made in a world where time flows only in the direction we are aware of, it is very interesting to imagine his theories when they are applied to a reverse-direction universe. In that context, a "cold death" scenario for the end of our cosmos becomes easier to imagine as the birthplace for a simultaneously existing reverse-time universe.

Physicist and Nobel laureate Richard Feynman proposed an interesting quantum physics concept which he called the "path integral method". Also known as the "sum over histories" or "sum over paths" approach, it suggests that any currently observed state for a particle does not have one but a great many ways that it could have arrived at its currently observed state. If we take that concept to our current discussion, we arrive at another conclusion that will take some getting used to. If we can imagine a series of yes-no decisions that get us from the big bang to the current reality any one of us are now experiencing, that is only one of many paths that could have been taken. In other words, that multitude of branches that is presented through our choices, chance, and the actions of others, which becomes all of the possible futures laid out before us at this moment, is only

Four – The Binary Viewpoint

half the story. There are an equally large number of fifth-dimensional paths that could have converged to arrive at this current moment, even though each of us are aware of only one of them from our limited fourth-dimensional awareness.[7]

Feynman's "sum over paths" method of calculation is now a commonly used shortcut for quantum physicists who are calculating the current path or position of a particle. When all the possible paths for a subatomic particle are averaged out, one path will emerge as the most likely to have happened, even though there are many other less likely paths which the particle could possibly have taken. In cosmological terms, this theory can potentially be expanded to show that the reason we are currently experiencing the universe we are in is because it is the most likely one to have sprung from initial conditions, even though there are many other less likely states which the universe could possibly be in. And, as we've already mentioned, Everett's Many Worlds concept tells us that all those other universes do, in fact, exist. Taken to human terms, the sum over paths method suggests that each of us have an infinite number of places in the universe that we could be, but that there is only one location that has the highest probability at any given moment. Interestingly, though, this means the theory predicts that there is still a possibility of other more unlikely occurrences to happen: there is no way to rule out the possibility that one of us could at this moment suddenly pop out of existence here and reappear on the moon. While the chances of that really happening are so small that it might take longer than the lifespan of the universe for such an event to occur, it also has to mean that it could happen

---

[7] As we discussed in the previous chapter, this is also a question of fifth dimensional trajectories. While it is true that there are many ways that we could have arrived at this current moment, there are also in our current moment certain futures that would be more likely to happen based upon what has happened so far. So, a different past which happens to arrive at the current reality we are now observing at this instant would have a different set of future moments that are more likely to occur, and some of those future moments would be extremely unlikely to occur from our own current timeline.

Four – The Binary Viewpoint

tomorrow. Like playing any lottery, it's just a question of the odds, no matter how one-sided they may be.

From the binary viewpoint, the tenth dimension becomes like the hugest computer memory in the world, containing every possible "0" and "1" that could be combined together to describe every possible universe. The "holodeck" of Star Trek: The Next Generation fame started out as a "simple" virtual reality simulator, but as the writers developed the series, its power appeared to grow to the point where entire universes could be created within its walls. How would a person's life inside such a world be different from a life in the real world? The somewhat confusing Matrix Trilogy started out with the same clear and profound concept–our experience inside a system capable of simulating every aspect of reality would, to our senses, be indistinguishable from the experience of actual reality.

Cosomologist Jacob Bekenstein estimates that if you were to digitize all aspects of the universe as we know it, it would take approximately 10^{100} bits of data. That's the number one followed by one hundred zeroes! So, if you were to have data storage in your computer equal to that amount, it might appear that you should be able to re-create and search through all aspects of the universe. It's amusing to note that particular number, one followed by one hundred zeroes, has a name that was coined by Milton Sirotta in 1937: he called it a "googol". That word is commonly spelled "google" today. Is this a coincidence? It would seem we have revealed the ultimate goal of the world's most popular search engine–that all aspects of the universe will be catalogued and searchable within its google-sized confines.

In 1997 the Argentinian physicist Juan Maldacena came up with an extrapolation of string theory that showed how a version of the universe could be imagined which is actually a gigantic hologram. This concept has triggered much new excitement in the world of theoretical physics, as it may offer easier ways of calculating the mathematics of string theory, and new ways of explaining gravity. But apart from all that, it's also just plain fun to think about how it offers us another Matrix-like view of reality: what is the difference between an actual physical universe and one that is holographically generated? The answer, cosmologists tell us, is that there would be no difference at all.

So, are we analogous to computing devices operating inside a gigantic memory chip of virtually infinite size? And is every entity that might be called a quantum observer actively choosing from the list of yes and no choices that indeterminacy sets before them at any particular instant? This is one of the biggest questions we can ask about this whole theory: if all we are talking about is a constant throwing of the dice with no interactivity, no qualitative decision making, no desire for things to be "this way instead of that way", then the entire construct we are examining here has no point whatsoever. If every event is completely random, right from the subatomic particles that happen to be selected by observation at any instant, to the massive infinities upon infinities we have imagined as we move up towards the tenth dimension, then why should we even discuss any of this?

This is what it comes down to: if we are willing to accept that we are creatures with free will who are moving through a fifth dimensional branching system of constant choices that then define–for each of us–the fourth dimensional timeline we experience, then to whatever extent that it matters, we must also be choosing the subatomic states that agree with the choices we are making. In other words, we are doing more than just "throwing the dice" in our role as quantum observers, and in fact each of us are actively influencing the outcome through the choices we make. We'll explore this more in chapter nine, "How Much Control Do We Have?".

Finally, the binary viewpoint can fail to take into account that there are usually three rather than two choices available for any situation involving free will: we can act (a "yes"), we can act in the opposite way (a "no"), or we can choose to do nothing. Any time we choose to do nothing, one of the other options may eventually be chosen for us, either by chance or by the actions of others. Sometimes this third option results in things turning out just fine, in which case we may "thank our lucky stars" or say a prayer of thanks. But any time we leave our choices up to this third option, we had best assure ourselves that we would be happy with either outcome.

Four – The Binary Viewpoint

FIVE–MEMES, MUSIC AND MEMORY

All living things carry within them quantum observers, collapsing the indeterminate wave of the "many worlds" multiverse into the universe we see around us. In the history of our universe, when did chemical reactions make the transition to life? One answer might be "when they began to exhibit an ability or desire to propagate and continue". Is the universe aware of itself? Are the genes that make up life aware of their long-term desire to continue? Does the planet earth have a self-organizing desire to continue, a Gaia consciousness? What about seemingly inanimate objects around us–does a rock or a mountain have any long time slow-moving spark of awareness within itself?

From 1976 to the present day, evolutionary biologist Richard Dawkins has written a series of books which advance the idea of the "Selfish Gene" swimming in a "River Out of Eden". His provocative viewpoint is that we are all "gene machines": the overarching reason for life to exist is to promote the continuation of certain genes from one generation to the next, and this process can be traced back to the beginning of life. As it turns out, the idea of individual genes as the defining influence in evolution has proved to be a more complex issue than it was thought when Dawkins first advanced his theories, as it is becoming apparent that genes work more like the lines of code in a complicated computer program rather than a simple set of on-off switches.

Still, Dawkins' viewpoint is fascinating to contemplate: in the long view of time, certain sets of genes have risen to prominence, could it be because of their desire to do so? This issue brings to mind all sorts of ramifications. Let's again take 9/11/01 as an example. When a set of genes from Afghanistan organizes the hijacking of airplanes to be used as suicide weapons against predominantly white Americans, is that an example of one gene set wanting to eliminate another? Would those innocent Muslims around the world who have been persecuted since then—even though they had nothing to do with the hijackings or the political motivations behind them—feel outrage because it seems it is their gene sets that are being attacked? In fact, any historical action which has targeted a specific set of genes for elimination (Hitler and the Holocaust being an extreme example from the twentieth century, for instance) might be a continuation of a long line of struggles for dominance of one gene set over another.

Richard Dawkins, of course, was advancing a theory which gave us a new way of looking at hundreds of millions of years of evolution rather than modern society, but it is interesting to apply the same "selfish gene" analysis to current events.

Dawkins also advanced the idea of the "meme" (rhymes with "team"), which would be an idea that desires itself to continue in the same way that a gene does. Ideas, belief systems, and unique points of view transfer themselves through word of mouth, the media, and so on. But the idea of the meme can also be stretched a bit to include more mysterious modes of transmission, where ideas seem to pop up simultaneously at geographically unrelated points.

Five – Memes, Music and Memory

Sometimes it seems that an idea is just "ready to be born", and that it may actually be somehow travelling across the fourth dimension and above without any visible mode of transmission. For instance, could this be a way to explain the coincidences of inspiration in scientific research, where unconnected people on opposite sides of the planet sometimes come up with the same groundbreaking theory or invention?[8]

One particularly infectious "meme" is contained within the Julian Jaynes book "The Evolution of Consciousness in the Breakdown of the Bicameral Mind". This innovative and challenging work advances the theory that self-awareness, that is to say, consciousness, is a relatively recent development in human history, perhaps only within the last few thousand years. Prior to that time, Mr. Jaynes contends, our conscious and subconscious minds were integrated, and we heard suggestions for future action from our subconscious mind as a voice or voices that we often interpreted as messages from the gods or departed loved ones.

---

[8] Actually, the idea of "simultaneous inspiration" being a common occurrence would itself be an example of a self-propagating meme. Here, in no particular order, are some examples of ideas which appear to have been discovered almost simultaneously by independent researchers and inventors: the phonograph, the light bulb, X-Rays, the telephone, non-Euclidean geometry, insulin, calculus, anesthesia, jet propulsion, topology, the airplane, the theory of evolution, the multiplying calculator, and the semiconductor laser. The discussion of the processes which led to those simultaneous occurrences is complicated. With some technologies, like the light bulb or the telephone, it can be argued that these discoveries filled a need which was already evident, and that the technology of the times had reached a point where those inventions were inevitable. In other cases, like the independent development of calculus by Newton and Leibniz, what you have are two completely different methodologies for arriving at the same results, which is why those two competing systems both continued to be taught for two hundred years after their invention. And of course, there are examples where there may have been actual theft of ideas – a favourite example is Alexander Graham Bell, who on February 14 1876 filed what was to become the most lucrative patent ever issued, for the telephone. Two hours later, Elisha Gray filed his own patent application for a telephone. Simultaneous inspiration? The big difference between the two patents was that Gray's invention included a "variable resistance transmitter" which was key to the functionality of the device. Bell had never even experimented with a variable resistance transmitter by the time he filed his patent. And yet, at some later date, a scribbled note was allowed to be added to the margin of Bell's patent which laid claim to this important enhancement.

Nonetheless, the notion of "ideas which are just out there", waiting to be plucked from above by those persons who are ready to receive them, has many proponents.

Five – Memes, Music and Memory

We still often exist in that more integrated state of mind, where we live within the moment rather than create an inner monologue watching and describing to ourselves what it is we're doing. Sometimes, interestingly enough, we *must* exist in that more integrated state of mind because otherwise there are tasks we would find ourselves incapable of doing. This is particularly true of any complicated physical action: if we are playing a musical instrument, or driving a car, or hitting a baseball, we do these things much better when repetition and the honing of our skills allow us to perform all the tiny actions that make up the activity without having to think about each of them. This has often been shown to be true of great mental achievements as well, where some of the finest minds of our time have reported that their important breakthroughs "just came to them", or even just "appeared in a dream".[9] In other words, this theory suggests that splitting our mental processes into a conscious mind which is constantly viewing our actions as if from the outside is not always a useful way to exist, and is not the way that most living organisms exist.[v]

Our consciousness is a multi-layered system, comprised of a variety of stored inputs and competing patterns, beliefs and innate actions. Marvin Minsky's book "The Society of Mind" is a wonderful exploration of this area of research, filled with groundbreaking insights and presented in a unique package. It should be made clear that Minsky does not use the Dawkins concept of "memes" in his book, and that experts schooled in Minsky's areas of research would probably take issue with the more generalized approach we are using here. Obviously, "Society of Mind" is a much more in-depth analysis of the specific mechanisms of intelligence and consciousness, while "memes" is a more

---

[9] The concept of "where creative inspiration comes from" is also held within this idea: many composers, writers, and artists have voiced the opinion that the forces for creativity are just "out there" waiting for anyone who is receptive to reach up and pluck an idea from this all-pervading ether that each of us are swimming in every day. Placing oneself in a frame of mind where one is more open to these creative memes that surround us from the higher dimensions seems to come more easily for some than others, but it should be something that any of us are capable of.

general concept which Dawkins intended to be used for the analysis of how ideas move and propagate through time. In this text we are deliberately blending those two approaches together, with apologies to either camp for any confusions about these individual schools of thought which may result.

Viewed as a set, one could describe the many memes that make up an individual as being their personality, or their way of looking at the world. One might also call this set of memes the soul. A common assumption is that each of us has a single soul which we carry with us from conception to death. But consider this: if we were to meet up with our own younger self from twenty years ago, what are the chances that we would share the same set of memes? It should be obvious that the chances of direct correlation are virtually nil. According to this line of reasoning, the illusion that a single body contains a single "soul" is a fiction. Each of us is a dynamic system, mutating and developing over time. Certainly, there is a core set of physical memories that will be encoded over time into each of our brains that will create links from past to present to future unique to each of us. But the memes and belief systems that make up our "soul" are much more complicated and transcendent across time and space than the set of physical memories each of us carries in our neurons. The memory of "What I Had for Lunch Last Thursday" will stretch out across time only for as long as any individual's brain cells recall it. Larger belief systems and emotions that make a person unique can extend well beyond the death of a body, and would be what survives, while the niggling details of day-to-day life would not.

Still, the physical body does provide each of us with a vessel in which those memes and memories collect, so its importance should not be minimized. Remember imagining ourselves as a fourth dimensional creature that resembled an undulating snake? Each instant that we look in the mirror we are seeing a three dimensional cross-section of that creature. We also imagined that the branches of choice and circumstance that affect each of us from moment to moment would represent multiple branches of that snake, as it divided itself across the fifth dimension. But what would that creature appear as in the sixth dimension? Like a physically real three-dimensional object built from its component parts in the first and second dimension, we don't really see a complete picture of our bodies until we reach the sixth dimension. The physical creature that represents every possible branch from the moment of conception to the final death of the oldest possible version of a particular person would, in the sixth dimension, be a fully-rounded, fully-textured representation drawn from every possible world-line that person could have experienced in the fourth and fifth dimension.

Parts of that shape would represent unfortunate paths where the person died in the womb, or where the person was stricken with a fatal childhood disease. Other parts would represent very fortunate paths where the person lived a long and happy life. Overall, each shape would have thicker sections which would represent the most likely world-lines to have occurred for that person, and that thickness would represent the many more choices that presented themselves to the numerous versions of that person from day to day: but the other less likely paths would also still be there, represented as feathering and tiny threads that spin off from the central mass.

An important question to ask is: if each of us has a version of ourselves that lives the longest and happiest life, why is that most often not the life that we end up experiencing? This is a complex issue, which we will spend a lot more time discussing in the chapter "How Much Control Do We Have?".

So, in the sixth dimension we can imagine two interlocking systems. There is physical reality as we experience it down here in the third dimension: the multiple branches possible for that physical reality can be viewed in their entirety as shapes within the sixth dimension. The other interlocking web in the sixth dimension is the system of beliefs and memes that each of us draw into and around ourselves to become a unique personality. Parts of that system of beliefs will extend back through our lifetime, attached to our physical bodies through memory to become a feeling of "self" that may not ever change. But, as we have already discussed, there are also parts of that system of beliefs that will constantly be in flux, altering over time as life experience changes the ways that a person thinks about themselves and the world.

We could think of this constantly changing system as a "society of memes". Like Minsky's concept of consciousness and intelligence, there will always be a large number of memes within each physical body which are competing for dominance, and which are brought to the forefront or suppressed depending upon their relevance and usefulness at any particular moment. It is the physical being we have been since conception, combined with that interlocking system we think of as our soul, that entwine in the sixth dimension to create an ornate and highly textured shape that is each of us, and which we see only a tiny cross-section of as we move along our line in the fourth dimension.

The beautiful blossoming potential we see in a newborn child is an immensely attractive thing. The angels of possibility that swirl around a toddler's head can be breathtaking if we catch even a fleeting glimpse. And there is nothing as sad as the tragedy of a child who has been mistreated or abused, and whose life may never be the same because of it. Even from our limited window in the lower dimensions, it is easy for us to intuitively understand what is magical and wonderful about the promise of a child, a promise that is held within the sixth dimension.

Perhaps we should take a breath for a moment and imagine once again how extraordinarily extravagant we already know our universe to be. As complex as what we have just pictured for ourselves may be, there is one more related layer that we can still also imagine. We have to appreciate that there could be many other genetically similar human beings which could have resulted (and, in the higher dimensions, did result) from a different sperm fertilizing our mother's egg just a few minutes earlier or later than the instant of our own conception. Like identical twins separated at birth that go on to have very similar life-paths, there would be other brothers or sisters that could have been born instead of you, that would have experienced the same environment and circumstance as you, and would therefore be physically separate beings in the sixth dimension who could nonetheless share an almost identical personality or set of memes. This, of course, gets into the old "nature versus nurture" debate, and just how many of those other genetically similar people you believe will end up with similar lives to your own has a lot to do with how much you believe either nature or nurture is the larger influence.

The question, then, of what makes each of us unique becomes blurred when we imagine how many similar versions of ourselves there could be in the higher dimensions, and how many similar conscious entities there could be that share the same set of memes. Admittedly, the more common belief that each person has a single and distinct "soul", carried with them for their entire life is at odds with the picture we are imagining here. Instead, we have a more fluid concept where the unique set of memes that currently make up a person could be shared by many others to greater and lesser extents, and could move from one person to another across time and space.

The connection that a group of like-minded people share (whether it be families, special interest groups, corporate culture, religion, sports fans, that song or band whose lyrics seem to express our innermost thoughts... this could be a very long list) can be viewed as a set of memes which connect people, not only in the third and fourth dimension but across higher dimensions as well.[vi] In this way, memes can be shown to be even more influential than genes because of their ability to extend so powerfully across time. For example, the words of a Chinese philosopher from 3500 years ago can still have the power to establish "viruses of the mind" which infect new readers and spread from person to person. Influential thinkers such as Confucius or Socrates set into motion memes which can continue to have their full effect even to this day. Conversely, the unique set of genes belonging to Confucius or Socrates (if they are even in the world's gene pool today), by now are so completely diluted as to be inconsequential.

A particular meme-set, when it is attached to a physical body, is the quantum observer for that person, collapsing the wave of possibilities along the arrow of time and experiencing life as we know it. However, since that set of memes can also be thought of as existing completely separately from a physical body, there are many other ramifications to this.

It is often theorized that ghosts are souls who have decided not to move on, but instead have decided to remain on the same current timeline. Some may have been unable to accept that their bodies are no longer alive, possibly because of a sudden unexpected death. Others might just be so interested in wanting to see "what happens next" that they continue in their role as observers long past the death of their own body. Viewed as an organized set of memes that move freely across time and space, it becomes easier to imagine how that unique "way of looking at the world" that makes up any individual could, just with the strength of its will to continue, manage to stay focused on our current reality, continuing to collapse the quantum wave function through observation even though the body they occupied is no longer animate.

The opposite is also true: many of us are painfully familiar with the experience of watching a loved one who, due to illness, extreme depression, or simple old age, have had their soul material gradually dissipate or be ground away. This can reach the point where we can see that the person that used to occupy that body is no longer there, even though the body continues to function. Where did they go? Perhaps they really did lose coherence and drift away. Or, more likely, most of the meme-set that made up that person lost interest in the diseased and tired body they were in and has already freed itself from its confines.

Five – Memes, Music and Memory

Witnessing the death of any living creature shows us one of the great mysteries of the universe: what leaves the body? Even something as simple as an apple, long after it has been picked from the tree, has processes of life that continue on within it, and which are passed on to those who consume it. Day after day, a bowl of apples on the counter will continue to carry that lifeforce within them. But eventually there comes a day when we can see than an apple has lost that intangible something, and as it dies the healthful benefits of eating that apple will quickly diminish.

How is it that we can so clearly see when the spark has departed, and a beautiful living thing becomes an inanimate lump of flesh? What we are describing here, then, should not be taken lightly: the amazing process that allows a set of memes and beliefs to occupy a living body and drive it forward—both with simple chemical desires to continue, and with higher processes of motivation and belief—truly is one of the most fantastic aspects of what we are describing here.

Still, bringing to mind a deceased loved one is bringing to mind some aspect of the meme-set that made up that person's personality, and which, in life, made that person who they were. So, in a very real sense, a part of that person can stay with us for as long as we can vividly recall what made that person unique and special to us at a certain time.[vii] Obviously, if that person were a meme-set that had continued to focus on our current timeline in a ghostly or spirit-like fashion, then that effect would be even more powerful.

So, if one of us were to meet a person we'd never seen before who shared virtually the same set of memes, are we meeting another incarnation of ourselves? If what defines each us as a being is our "way of looking at the world", then that particular system would exist freely across time and space, and the thought of reincarnations being limited to other times becomes an unnecessary restriction. Why couldn't other incarnations of you be walking the earth at the same time as you are right now?

Likewise, if we were to vividly recall what our own thoughts and feelings from twenty years ago had been, we would be able to re-activate that "way of looking at the world": another form of reincarnation. Strong memories like these are often triggered by our senses, a process we will explore more in chapter eight.

Here's another way to look at this idea: if each of us has a unique soul, where are all the new souls coming from? Our planet's population has exploded in numbers, so there must be new "soul material" being created from somewhere. In the New Age community, theories abound regarding what that source might be. All of those theories may be held within the version of reality that we are advancing here: if our soul is a conglomeration of memes that exist outside of time, then other versions of that soul could exist in other universes, in other locations within our universe, in other parts of the history and future of our universe, and even right now in other parts of our own world. The idea that it's possible to meet another incarnation of yourself right now may take some getting used to, but it is an important aspect of the version of reality we are exploring.

Admittedly, the discussion of supernatural topics such as ghosts and reincarnation falls into territory which some readers are not comfortable with, so we will not dwell on this any more at present. Nonetheless, these ideas hold important ramifications, and we'll touch on them again in some of the upcoming chapters.

In different kinds of music, we are usually able to analyze the style and emotional content of a piece by looking at different layers and their relationship to each other. Many of these layers define the "groove" (this term is most often used to refer to popular music styles, but as a form of musical analysis it can be applied in various ways to much more than that). A piece of music will have a certain density of fast notes or slow notes, grouped together in various ways, each grouping having various cultural or emotional resonances which are well outside the scope of this present discussion. It will have a "breath" (defined by the length of individual phrases) and a "heartbeat" (usually defined by the metronomic pulse of the piece). It will have longer structures which tend to repeat in ways that are either jarring, soothing, or invigorating, depending upon the intent and structure of the piece–from something so simple as the verse/chorus/bridge of a hit tune, to the intricately interlocking layers of a Bach fugue, and so on.

It's entirely possible to enjoy a piece of music without being consciously aware of these structures, but many musicologists would argue that we as human beings tend to respond to these subtleties even without being aware of their existence. With the more subtle nuances of groove, it's conceivable that a less sensitive person might be incapable of appreciating the unusual swing value or several millisecond push before the beat that a certain performer might be adding to their part, but that listener would still be able to enjoy the more big-picture aspects of a particular piece of music, such as its heartbeat and breath. In other words, different people can listen to the same piece of music and appreciate completely different things about it, and each viewpoint is valid in its own way.

Likewise, the emotional content of a piece of music is derived not just from the piece itself but by the resonances and contrasts that piece has with other compositions.

If a song were a life, there would be interesting parallels. Different people, presented with the same song, might draw completely different things from what is presented to them. A song will have many connections to other songs, and it is those resonances and repetitions which bring a certain piece of music its power and its emotion. And it is the contrast of one song to the next that makes us appreciate many others.

In terms of consciousness, songs provide us with a way of thinking of how one person could have many different aspects to their being which exist at different levels, some of them very fast-moving and dense, some of them very long or intermittent. Think of one of your favourite songs from ten years ago. Now think of every time you have heard that song since then, and the connections in time and space that were made every time that song came back. This is an example of a longer groove than most of us are used to thinking about. But the interlocking system of beliefs and instinct that make up an individual can stretch across time much further than the duration of a single life: trying to imagine what it would feel like to be one of those much longer timespan systems is an interesting exercise.

Graham Hancock, in his book "The Mars Mystery", tells of a system of mirrors that were left behind on the moon by the Apollo astronauts. From 1973 to 1976 researchers used a 107-inch telescope to direct more than 2,000 laser beams at these mirrors. These laser beams allowed extremely precise measurements to be made and revealed a 15-meter oscillation of the lunar surface about its polar axis, with a period of about three years. Astronomer David Levy suggested that the moon is behaving "just like a huge bell after it has been clanged". Scientists proposed that this must be the result of a relatively recent major impact, and that this ringing will die out after 20,000 years or so. Imagine, now, that you are somehow able to slow down your awareness to the point where you are able to hear the ringing of that bell.[viii]

Admittedly this all starts to sound like a Zen koan, and in some ways the goal is the same—we are trying to free ourselves from a limited viewpoint of the universe and the nature of time.

Normally we feel we are experiencing time as a vector moving in a specific direction. But there are times when that is not the case, where our experience becomes timeless, or where time seems to move very slow or very fast. If time is like a Möbius strip, where the twists and turns we make in the dimensions above still appear as a straight line in the dimension below, than we can imagine how our fourth dimensional "straight" line of time is a really a curving and branching line in the fifth dimension. An experience of time, the fourth dimension, that feels slow and boring to us might be seen as more of a series of squiggles in the fifth dimension that therefore advance more slowly in what we think of as "time". An idea, or meme, that spreads quickly might be describing a line in the fifth dimension that is almost at right angles to our fourth dimensional line of time, so that rather than running almost parallel to our perceived progress in the fourth dimension it joins points quickly in the third dimension (space), to become an idea that quickly sweeps the world.

We all have parts of our day where we are completely unaware of the passage of time. In the Julian Jaynes point of view, these would be the parts of our day when the "narrator voice" of our consciousness ceases its constant monologue, and we merge back into the unified point of view of our ancestors, and, indeed, of most other living things. At those moments, we continue to act as quantum observers, but there is nothing remarkable about the process to stick in our memory.

What we do remember are the moments where an important branch occurred in the "straight" line of our fourth dimensional experience. Thinking fifth-dimensionally, our personal timeline (or "world-line") might be proceeding uneventfully, but then we reach the moment where a major decision, a random event, or the actions of others resulted in a blossoming or a branching extending out from that "straight" line of our life-path. Everyone remembers what they were doing the moment they saw the World Trade Center towers collapse. Everyone remembers the day they won a big prize or the day they saw a loved one die. And even with perfect strangers, we are drawn to the moments we recognize as being important cusps in that person's life. This is why it is human nature to want to drive slowly by the car accident, trying to catch a glimpse of what happened, or why we all will look at the newspaper picture of the latest lottery winner. No matter whether the event was good or bad, fortunate or unfortunate, we all have a tendency to think "what if that had been me?".[ix]

Well, someplace out there in the sixth dimension, all those things did happen to you. Good and bad, fortunate and unfortunate, there is another you who is dealing with that particular timeline, or who has died trying.

Haitian Voodoo has an interesting sidebar to this concept. The deities in this religion are "loas" who can ride human beings around as if they are horses, taking over the bodies and actions of whoever they choose. Now, ask yourself this: if you were able to ride a different "you" from the one you are on right now, how would that person be different? This becomes a question of self-actualization and an exploration of the power of positive thinking, which some will immediately shy away from as being self-deceiving drivel. We'll explore these concepts more in chapter nine, but for now let's just think about it this way. By imagining how you want to change yourself, you can imagine a path that you would have to follow to become that person. In other words, you imagine a series of branches in the fifth dimension which allow you to change and grow. We all have to recognize that there are branches that are impossible to get to because they would require a leap through the sixth dimension, but that still leaves a huge range of fifth dimensional paths which each of us truly can get to from where we are at this moment. We are all travellers in the fifth dimension, each of us drawing a fourth dimensional line with our three dimensional bodies.

Sometimes people get caught in loops of addiction and abuse that trap them into circles, causing them to go back again and again to bad relationships, alcohol, or other drugs, with a feeling that there's no way out. This is one of the pitfalls that the fifth dimension can set for people, as it offers an easy path to fold back to the same negative repetitions over and over again. There's not much to say about this except that the fifth dimension offers many paths for escape as well, and the hardest part of the problem is usually identifying what is triggering the negative repetition and finding a way to break the pattern.[x] Unquestionably, this is a serious issue, and anyone who is having to deal with the negative repercussions of an addiction of any kind should seek help wherever they can find it. The good news is, there are always multiple fifth-dimensional paths available, and the one that leads back into the negative repetition is never the only option.

In the chapter "The Flow of Time" we imagined life as we know it springing from processes which happen to occur in one direction. What we didn't spend time exploring then is the concept that the first spark of life could therefore be thought of as being the result of a quantum observer choosing one path over another, resulting in that particular chemical process appearing to express a "desire to continue". If you go back to the primordial stew from which our planet and then life evolved, it would seem that you will have to establish some point in time at which you say: "this was a group of chemical reactions which had a potential tendency towards self-replication", then a little bit later: "and this is the beginning of life". What is the dividing line? And does it matter where the dividing line is? Perhaps the idea of the beginning of life is another one of those concepts which reflects our own limited viewpoint. If life is just a desire to continue, then some form of awareness–a quantum observer of some description–should be able to be traced back to the beginning of the unique big bang which reflects our own fortuitous universe.[10]

The role of the quantum observer in the creation of a universe–whether it be one of the hospitable ones such as we find ourselves lucky enough to occupy, or one of the difficult universes which quickly collapses back in upon itself or flies apart into disorder–is an interesting conundrum. If there were no observer to collapse a

---

[10] Countless science fiction authors, of course, have presented us with many thought-provoking ways of imagining other lifeforms. Stephen Baxter, in a mythos he has developed across his "Xeelee Sequence" and "Destiny's Children" series of books, has helped us to imagine entire races and civilizations which may have evolved and faded within the ultra-high-energy first few milliseconds of the big bang. Conversely, Baxter has shown us what it might be to become a slow-moving being in the low energy/high entropy end of the universe, where the formation of a single thought might take thousands of years. And Greg Bear, in novels such as "Legacy" and "Blood Music" describes in vivid detail vast ecologies which could have developed as a result of life finding other completely different ways to manifest itself.

Five – Memes, Music and Memory

"difficult" universe out of the potential held within the tenth dimension, then does that difficult universe exist or not?

Likewise, even in our modern existence in a fortunate universe, on a planet teeming with life, the possibilities of branching from one moment to the next are virtually endless. It would seem that this theory must be implying that there is a version of reality about to happen where any one of us now suddenly snaps and goes on a murderous rampage! Surely, with all the possible universes that could exist one second from now, there must be a high percentage where a particular combination of choices is not taken?

We'll return to aspects of this discussion more in the next few chapters. But for now, let's look at it this way: how is there a difference between a universe that could potentially have existed and one that actually exists? The only difference is whether a quantum observer was there to collapse that reality into existence through observation. As we've already briefly touched upon, this is one of the interpretations of the "anthropic principle": all of those other difficult or unlikely universes exist, there just aren't creatures like ourselves within those universes to ask the questions we are asking.

As we've explored in this chapter, there are many more ways for the quantum observer to express itself than within any one single life. In other words, the integrated systems of belief, dreams, and choice which are interacting with a physical world of life, DNA, and molecules are all floating across fourth-, fifth-, and sixth-dimensional time and space in much longer and wider paths than the limited viewpoint each of us experience as a single life moving along the "line of time" within our physical bodies.

As quantum observers, we are all participating in a rich tapestry of experience that becomes consensual reality for each of us. But as rich as that tapestry may appear to be, it is still only a tiny subset of all the possible realities, and the potential for those realities is contained within the tenth dimension.

Five – Memes, Music and Memory

SIX-THE ANTHROPIC VIEWPOINT

One of the most common arguments used to debunk evolution or to prove the existence of an Intelligent Creator-God is to simply point at how impossibly complex our universe, our world, and we as creatures living in it all really are. How could something as wonderful as the eye of an eagle ever have evolved? The intermediate steps between "no eye" and "an eye capable of spotting tiny prey from high flight" are difficult to imagine if they are purely the result of random chance and natural selection. It would be like imagining a television just happening to evolve from random parts in a junkyard without any human intervention. This common sense viewpoint could be summed up as "the existence of a creation demands a creator".

An answer to this question which is advanced by cosmologists is called the "anthropic principle". This concept could be summed up by an equally simple phrase: "the reason we're here is because we're here".[xi] In other words, the reason we're here to ask questions about the seemingly impossible odds against our own existence as a result of billions of years of good luck, fortuitous choices, and natural selection is because if we hadn't beat the odds we wouldn't be here to ask the question. And, as we've described before, the anthropic principle is often used to go further into the multi-dimensional version of reality that we're discussing in this text: all of those other universes that didn't have the good fortune to create stars, planets, and intelligent life do actually exist, but don't have intelligent occupants to ask how they happened to be there.

There are many ways we can play with the anthropic principle. For instance, it is also useful for imagining why we are never visited by alien civilizations or time travellers from the future (assuming, of course, that we all believe these things haven't happened). From the anthropic viewpoint, we can say that those events have occurred, but not on our timeline–they are part of another of the possible universes, but not ours. So the universe where a time traveller went back to 1963 and threw himself in front of JFK's limo at the exact right moment to prevent the assassination does exist, but that's not the universe we're in. The universe also exists where an alien civilization arrived here yesterday, but they were so hopelessly advanced that they viewed us much as we might view an anthill and destroyed humanity without thinking about it: in that universe, right now, we're all dead.

These arguments are sometimes dismissed as being too convenient, as they allow a carte blanche approach to explaining away virtually anything. However, we should keep in mind that the wonderfully complex and horribly inequitable world we live in is just as unlikely as any of the scenarios we've just described, and that an observer from outside our timeline would find the improbable occurrences which led to this moment in time to be just as outrageously unlikely as any of the other timelines we could care to imagine.

The unlikely nature of any particular timeline is what the anthropic principle is all about. Let's think about some of the unlikely timelines which could have happened in our past but for whatever reason appear to have never occurred.

Six – The Anthropic Viewpoint

It seems that no matter where you are in history, at a specific moment there will always be a certain small contingent of the population who are predicting the end of the world. Usually it's some conveniently distant amount of time away from the present to be a cause for concern, but not so close as to immediately leave the person spreading the news with egg on their face (as I write this in 2006, the Mayan calendar's December 21 2012 looks like a good upcoming contender for an end-of-the world focal point some portion of the public are likely to become caught up with).

But eventually the deadline for all good predictions of the end has to arrive, and like the celebrated Y2K scenario, its promoters are then left looking a little foolish. In the anthropic viewpoint, we can imagine how those people also exist on different timelines where their predictions did come true. The reason we're here on our current timeline to question what went wrong with their predictions is because on the timeline where they were right, we would no longer be here.[xii] Perhaps there were also people in Atlantis, or Mu/Lemuria, or in the ancient sunken ruins off of Cuba or south of Okinawa, who issued dire warnings of impending disaster, and who got to say one last "I told you so" before the end of their civilizations really did come to pass?

From the anthropic viewpoint, then, it seems we become like Schrödinger's Cat (see Illustration 12), simultaneously alive and dead. The fact that we don't actually perceive ourselves as being dead is because if we were dead we wouldn't be here to ask the question. The fact that you didn't win the last three lotteries is not because there isn't a universe where you did.

Don't you love triple negatives? This also appears to say "the fact that you didn't win the last three lotteries is because there is a universe where you did". While the version of the anthropic viewpoint we're favouring here tells us that is most certainly true, there is one important distinction we have to make.

Six – The Anthropic Viewpoint

Illustration 12 - SCHRODINGER'S CAT

Fig. 12-a

a. In 1935 Erwin Schrödinger proposed this thought experiment somewhat in jest to demonstrate the contradictions inherent in quantum indeterminacy when it is applied to the physical world. A live cat is sealed inside a box. Inside is a tiny bit of radioactive material and a Geiger counter, hooked up to an electrically activated hammer poised next to a vial of hydrocyanic acid. If a radioactive particle decays, the Geiger counter triggers the hammer which hits the vial and the fumes kill the cat.

b. Quantum physics has demonstrated that, until we actually observe the subatomic particle that might have decayed and set off the Geiger counter, both states will be true within the wave function of quantum indeterminacy. In other words, until our act of observation collapses one or the other outcome into existence, both outcomes exist. But following this line of reasoning, Schrödinger pointed out, leads us to the conclusion that, until we open the steel box and observe the result, the cat must be simultaneously alive and dead!

Fig. 12-b

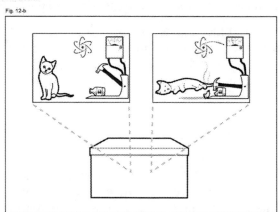

At the subatomic level, this effect is known as "superposition", and there are many experiments which have proven that a single particle can indeed be in multiple locations or states simultaneously. Whether superposition applies to the physical world has been an open debate now for many decades, and later in his life Schrödinger himself is rumoured to have said that he "wished he'd never met that cat".

Six – The Anthropic Viewpoint

As we discussed in chapter four, quantum indeterminacy tells us that there is a version of our world where any one of us now pops out of existence and reappears on Mars. Yes, the chances of that happening are statistically improbable, and the sum-over-path trajectory that might make that more likely to happen may not be the trajectory we are currently on. But what we have to keep in mind is that it is the *potential* for all of those other past and future events to occur that exists within the tenth dimension.

Granted, all of this can start to seem like nonsense unless you can find a way to accept that all the other possible universes do actually exist. It is for this very reason that the anthropic principle is sometimes dismissed as being too simplistic a concept, and ridiculed because it appears to be a dead end. Clearly, Everett's Many Worlds Theory is tied up into the interpretation of the anthropic principle which we are favouring here, but the idea of a virtually limitless number of other universes which are not part of our own universe is admittedly a large pill to swallow. Even if we choose to leave some of those other universes out, on the assumption that there are ones that no quantum observer ever collapses, we still are left with the challenging idea that within the tenth dimension we find the potential to exist for all of those other universes and all of their timelines.

The critics of the Anthropic Principle have an easily stated argument. Even if Stephen Hawking (in "The Universe in a Nutshell") and other great minds of our time have subscribed to this theory, so what? If these other alternate universes and realities exist, the detractors will say, then show them to me. Prove their existence.

So, once again, we get to a point in the discussion that becomes more like a question of faith. What do you choose to believe? If you've made it this far along I am hoping that you, dear reader, still at least have an open mind about the possibilities we are exploring here.[xiii]

Conspiracy theorists should love the anthropic viewpoint, because it implies that a very specific set of choices have been made to get us to the reality we currently live in. The reason certain families have money and power, the reason certain societies have been able to exert control over our destinies, is because of a long list of backroom deals and hidden skulduggery leading back through the ages. The fact that human beings evolved to become the dominant species might be a result of the "Secret Plan for the Advancement of Mammals". The fact that hydrogen became the most common element in our universe is, of course, because of the "Great Hydrogen Conspiracy", which stretches back to a mere 380,000 years after the Big Bang, when atoms first started to form. And most mysterious of all, the fact that Dark Matter and Dark Energy are by far the most predominant forms in the universe may be part of a plot that stretches out much further than our own Big Bang! In all of these examples, the anthropic viewpoint tells us that there are other universes where those conspiracies failed, and other factions rose to dominance. We just don't happen to be in those universes.

In chapter four we looked at the binary viewpoint, where we described the attempt to categorize everything into "on/off", or "these are the things something is/these are the things it isn't". In this chapter we are provided with a third-layer counterpoint to that way of thinking: it tells us that the lesson of quantum physics is that we can often view things as being (for example) "on, off, or simultaneously on and off", or (as another example) "a wave, a particle, or both a wave and a particle". Admittedly, this can leave us in a position like Mr. Schrödinger's poor cat, caught in a limbo somewhere between existence and non-existence as we imagine the higher dimensions. But the groups of three that are often implied within dualities—such as the dual nature of the tenth dimension and the eleventh dimension which modern physicists are exploring, for instance, or any other dualistic viewpoint—give us other ways of thinking which will continue to be useful to us throughout this text. Please keep this in mind as our discussion continues: we can often arrive at the idea of a third layer being implied by groups of two by combining the binary viewpoint with the anthropic viewpoint.[11] The fact that so much of what we are talking about ends up in groups of three will become more important as we reach our final chapters.

Admittedly, there is a certain fatalistic aspect to the anthropic viewpoint. The idea that each of us controls our own future through our own choices seems to be dwarfed by the immensity of the choices and random occurrences that have already taken place to get us from the beginning of time to where we are today, and the astronomically larger immensity of choices which will have created all of the other universes that we are not currently in. This, then, becomes another of those "order of magnitude" jumps that the brain has difficulty dealing with simultaneously. Yes, on the one hand the number of events and actions that have occurred to get us to current circumstance are huge and daunting in their complexity. On the other hand, the number of choices that each of us can continue to make each day, each with their own good or bad consequences, are also immense and diverse. In the anthropic viewpoint, the choices each of us make today will create one and only one anthropic universe tomorrow for each of us to live in, and that universe will be the direct result of the combined actions and inactions of today.

---

[11] Obviously this is not the only way to sum up this conclusions, it's just one that seems convenient within the discussion points we've been pursuing as we move from chapter to chapter. We could also say that we arrive at this by combining classical reality with Everett's Many Worlds theory, or by accepting the simultaneous wave/particle nature of reality which is implied by the probability function of quantum physics. These are all different ways of saying the same thing: that something that can be considered as being one way, and also another way, can sometimes also be considered as potentially being in both conditions simultaneously.

Six – The Anthropic Viewpoint

SEVEN—THE PARADOXES OF TIME TRAVEL

Now let's have a little fun. Time travel, according to modern physics, may theoretically be possible, but the energies involved in such a process are so beyond any technology we can currently imagine that it may always remain unattainable. In movies and literature, of course, time travel has long been a staple. What happens when we take the ten dimensional concepts we have established and apply them to these works of fiction?

Clearly, when we're talking about a piece of entertainment it's unfair to apply too deep of an analysis to a certain story or film, and criticize elements which have been put into the story for their dramatic impact rather than because of the author's desire to present a rigorous scientific viewpoint. What we're exploring here is merely a discussion of how the ramifications of a particular plotline might fit in with the tenth dimensional construct we've now established for ourselves, and this is intended only as an intellectual diversion, rather than an attempt to somehow belittle a particular work of fiction. As entertainments, these are stories and films that I love, and that I continue to enjoy even having analyzed them from the perspective of the ten dimensions.

"Back to the Future" is a popular example of a movie which, one could say, attempts to show what happens in the fifth dimension as a result of changes made in a fourth dimensional timeline. By changing some event at one point in time, it should be readily apparent that we "branch" to another possible future, which would no longer be on our current "straight" line, so our fourth dimensional line has branched into the fifth dimension. What may not be apparent from movies and stories dealing with the paradoxes of time travel is that those paradoxes can often be resolved if we find a way to incorporate the idea that all possible pasts and futures really do exist. As strange a concept as that may be to swallow, there is mounting theoretical evidence from quantum physics and string theory indicating that could actually be the case (please refer to the previously mentioned books by Randall, Greene and Kaku if you would like to know more about these theories).

The picture we have drawn for ourselves is that the fourth, fifth, and sixth dimensions together represent all the pasts and futures that could exist for our universe. This is a tricky concept for we human beings trapped in a point moving along a line in the fourth dimension to fully appreciate. Our eyes tell us there is only one world, and that world is already unfathomably complex, subtle and mysterious. How could there be anything more? From our individual perspective, when each of us makes a decision, all of the other possible consequences from the alternate decisions that had been available to us disappear like just so much fairy dust.

Again, this becomes another of those "order of magnitude" leaps which we can only take one step at time, because simultaneously imagining layers of this complexity is such a difficult task. Like the leap from atom to solar system, we have to accept that our poor brains are wired to be able to think about one and then the other, and that is about as much as we are generally able to process. So, no matter how beautiful and finely detailed we know the world we see around us is, we have to then "take a snapshot" of that reality, file it away in our minds, and move on to imagining how each possible branching of reality reflects an equally detailed snapshot, and that all of those snapshots of possible pasts and futures do actually exist simultaneously in the higher dimensions.

In the Terry Gilliam movie "Twelve Monkeys"[12] (spoiler warning, skip this paragraph if you don't want to be told how this movie ends) a boy witnesses a man being shot to death in the airport. Much later in the film we discover that the man shot was that same character as an adult who had travelled back in time to his own boyhood days. Here is an example of a time travel concept that at first blush might seem to be an impossible paradox, but in fifth dimensional thinking can easily be explained. If the boy in this version of history saw his own death, nothing about the boy's life from that moment changes, because in the boy's timeline he will always have witnessed his own death. But it's important to remember, once again, that this must also mean there is a universe where the man never travelled back in time and therefore was not killed in his boyhood days, another where the boy wasn't at the airport that day and therefore didn't witness his own death, plus others where the boy witnessed his adult self making a successful getaway, and so on.

Let's look a little more closely at Back to the Future. In this film, we see Michael J. Fox as Marty, a modern teenager who inadvertently travels back in time and meets his parents who are then teenagers themselves. Marty meets his own mother prior to her falling in love with his future-to-be father, and Marty's presence causes the series of events that led to their romance to be interrupted. Needless to say this becomes a concern to Marty because, as we discover, it

---

[12] Film buff purists would want us to note that "Twelve Monkeys" was inspired by a 28 minute French film released in 1962 by Chris Mark, called *"La Jetée"*.

prevents Marty from being born in the new timeline that his mother's life-path is branching to. Clearly, if all timelines exist this is not a big deal, as distasteful as that idea may be to Marty. But if he then wants to patch the relationship up and get his mother and father to fall in love under new and better circumstances, that is his also his prerogative. When he is successful yet another of the potential future timelines will be branched to, and that timeline would appear to be the one he travels upon when he returns to find his much-improved family at the end of the movie.

The parts of this story that don't make sense from the fifth/sixth dimensional perspective we've now established– as much fun as they were within the storyline–are when Marty is looking at family photographs with his image starting to fade, or when he himself appears to start dissolving when his parents are going to fail to get together. It appears there is no way within the story's world to explain why those events would happen without insisting there is somehow only one true timeline, only one fourth dimensional line that is allowed to exist. But if that is the case then Marty will always have travelled to his own past and his family's future will have always been the new improved version we see at the end of the movie, a conclusion which creates all sorts of annoying paradoxes. In the description of ten dimensions we are currently exploring, either one timeline can be viewed or the other: there is no blurry "half way between" timeline being predicted. But if we cannot buy into the idea that there are multiple fifth dimensional timelines, then we are herding ourselves into a corner where nobody in the world has free will, and we are all just acting on a predetermined script. What would be the point of living in such a universe?

This movie deals with a particular version of what is often referred to as the "grandfather paradox" in discussions of time travel: if a person goes back in time and kills their own grandfather, then that means the person didn't exist, which means they didn't go back in time to kill their own grandfather, which means they do exist after all, which means they can again go back in time... and around and around we spin in an endless loop.

It should be clearer now that "Back to A Future" might have been a better title for this movie trilogy, since anyone who goes into their own past will never be able to get back to the present they had started from–because in that present time they started from they had never travelled to their own past. Their action of travelling to the past automatically puts them on a new timeline, the one where they had been in their own past, which might end up arriving at a present extremely similar to their original timeline, but is more likely to be completely different. Paradoxes such as this are built into any discussion of time travel–but agreeing that all possible pasts and futures really do exist is still easier to deal with than the alternative, which would be to imagine that there is only one real timeline and every aspect of the past and future is already carved into stone. If each of us is correct in our belief that we have free will, then the future must be filled with options, not just a single track.

There could be a whole other set of "Back to A Future" movies created where the inherent paradoxes are explored–for instance there is the plot where Marty travels to the new and improved future (the ending of the original movie), and discovers a family and friends who have lived a happy life with some other "timeline twin" of Marty, who we will call "New Marty". "Old Marty" realizes that "New Marty" must exist, because otherwise his new and improved family wouldn't have recognized him, and would have chased him out of the house as a stranger. So "Old Marty" has a gruesome task ahead of him: he must find and kill "New Marty" and dispose of the body before anyone finds out they both exist. The rest of the movie would entertain us with the hilarious slip-ups as "Old Marty" then tries to interact with his new and improved family despite never having shared any of their past years together.

Stephen King, in his monolithic "Dark Tower" series offers an interesting compromise to this question–he proposes that there are indeed multiple timelines and multiple worlds of unfolding possibility, but there is also one "keystone" world where events are much more significant. He suggests that it will be no big deal if someone dies in the "other" timelines, but if someone dies in the keystone world then they are really and truly dead forever. While this is a useful literary device because it avoids the free-floating nature of exploring all fifth-dimensional timelines simultaneously, as a viewpoint it still creates more questions than it answers. How can one be certain that they are in the keystone world and not on some other less significant branch?[13] How should one react if they discover they are not in the keystone world, so their actions are not going to have as much consequence? What does it mean to be "truly" dead if many other versions of a person can continue to have long and happy lives in some of the other "non-keystone" timelines? Are we imagining that all evidence of a person's existence will inexplicably vanish in all the other worlds when they die in the keystone world, or that photographs of themselves will become semi-transparent in the other worlds if it looks like they're about to die in the keystone world? As with "Back to the Future", by following this line of reasoning we run the risk of being trapped in paradoxes. If there is only one true path for one keystone world, then how do we avoid saying that the path has always existed and therefore our own free will is pointless?

Discussions of free will crop up again and again as we imagine travelling in time. One theory that attempts to deal with this issue is known as the Novikov Self-Consistency Principle, which was developed by Igor Novikov of the University of Copenhagen. This theory starts with the

---

[13] To be fair, King talks about things seeming more real, less washed out when his characters jump into the keystone world. King's "keystone world" idea connects to the first, more limited interpretation of the anthropic principle, which also connects to the "river of time" concept which we will explore more later. Einstein echoed the same concept when he suggested that "God had no choice" in creating the universe: in other words, the extremely unlikely universe we live in is the only one that could have been created, because any others from different initial conditions would not support life as we know it. According to that interpretation, the river of time could only have flowed to the specific moment we are in now and no others, because the other rivers would have collapsed, disappeared, or dispersed into the ocean of entropy by now.

commonly held assumption that there is only one reality, and only one real time-line for the universe. Assuming that time travel becomes a possibility for us at some point, persons travelling in time to their own past would find it impossible to do anything that would create a paradox: in other words, even if they were to point a gun at their own grandfather, something would always happen to prevent the gun from firing, or the bullet would always miss. The most one could do would be to wound their own grandfather, so long as the wound did not prevent good ol' grampa from then having the child that becomes the time traveller's mother or father.

The mysterious force that would prevent the paradox of killing your grandfather from occurring would appear to be removing free will from the equation. Proponents of this theory point out that this is not that unusual: for instance, no matter how much we attempt to exercise our free will there are certain natural forces in our world, like gravity or the apparent solidity of a wall, that we are simply not able to overcome. In the scenario we're examining then, attempting to kill your grandfather would be like attempting to levitate or to walk through a wall: no matter how much you try, you are simply unable to do so. While Novikov's theory (which is also sometimes referred to as the Consistency Conjecture) does hold a certain fascination, it appears to be a completely unnecessary tangent if we are pursuing the world of quantum indeterminacy and the multiverse proposed by modern physics.

Certain authors are notable for their fifth- and sixth-dimensional approach: the large body of work of Philip K. Dick, for instance, represents numerous explorations of time and the relationship between reality and perception (admittedly some of his works do this more successfully than others). Madeline L'Engle's transcendent "A Wrinkle In Time" has introduced several generations of young readers to the concept of being able to "fold" time and jump to different realities, and unquestionably had a profound effect on my own way of thinking when I first read it at the age of eight.

But there are also well-known movies and works of fiction that deal with the multi-dimensional nature of reality without appearing to be science fiction. "It's a Wonderful Life" is one of the first examples of a popular movie which we could say introduced the public to a multi-dimensional way of thinking. By going back and viewing what George Bailey's world would have been like without him there, the angel Clarence would appear to have the ability to take people on jumps through the sixth dimension to other fifth-dimensional timelines.

We could even say "A Christmas Carol" has a multi-dimensional element to it, when Ebenezer Scrooge is shown one possible fifth-dimensional branch of his own future, then reforms his ways and enters a different fifth-dimensional path.

We are not for a moment suggesting that Charles Dickens or Frank Capra were attempting to promote a multiple-dimensional viewpoint of reality. Rather, we are exploring how these particular stories happen to have elements which can fit within the concepts we are exploring.

One of the best examples of such a story is the film "Groundhog Day", which introduced the public to a lovely dimensional puzzle: what would happen if, inexplicably, someone were forced every twenty-four hours to jump back through the sixth dimension to exactly the same fourth dimensional point in time, then explore one after another a gigantic sampling of all the fifth-dimensional branches which could have taken place from that moment onward—but with the added wrinkle that the person would continue to have knowledge of all the branches they had previously explored? We'll discuss this surprisingly insightful film some more in the chapter "How Much Control Do We Have?".

Granted, it would be easy to dismiss this entire discussion by simply saying "time travel is impossible, these are all works of fiction, so to worry about whether the logic of a particular movie or story's depiction of time travel is accurate is completely pointless". Nonetheless, it is not just science fiction authors but famous physicists who have postulated the concept of "wormholes" as a way to jump through space and time. A wormhole would be the equivalent of a "fold" in a higher dimension according to the theory we are exploring here, which means we'd be able to categorize what dimension the wormhole was "folding through" by the nature of the outcome. So, a wormhole that allowed you to jump to a different part of our current universe without the passage of time would be folding space, the third dimension, through the fourth dimension. A wormhole that allowed you to jump to a different part of our current timeline (our past or our future) would be folding time through the fifth dimension. A wormhole that allowed you to jump to a different past than the one we currently share would be folding "alternate space-times" (the fifth dimension) through the sixth dimension. And a wormhole that allowed you to jump to a completely different universe with different physical laws than our own would be folding our space-time through the seventh dimension (or above).

While it's certainly true that the technology to allow time travel and wormholes is beyond anything even remotely within the bounds of our current knowledge, the exponential increases in humanity's technological achievements over the last century may end up on a path in the decades or centuries to come that moves us closer to that capability much sooner than one might currently be able to expect. And regardless of whether time travel becomes a possibility any time soon, what we are discussing here is a theoretical way of imagining whether a particular story could somehow have any resonance with how the universe is constructed, as we imagine it from the perspective of ten dimensions. Speaking more generally, it's interesting how some works of fiction, no matter how unconnected they may be to one's personal experience, will have a ring of truth to them, while others pieces will seem hollow, lacking in resonance. Reading a work of fiction that puts you into the head of someone whose life is completely different from your own can be a powerful and moving experience.

Seven – The Paradoxes of Time Travel

For works of fiction dealing with time travel, I would like to believe that those which appear to be based upon there always only being one true timeline will always be less successful in achieving that deep resonance than those that acknowledge the multi-path nature of time. For every rule there are exceptions though, and I would have to say that Audrey Niffenegger's "The Time Traveller's Wife" is a superb example. Like Kurt Vonnegut's Billy Pilgrim from "Slaughterhouse Five", Niffenegger's book tells the tale of a man who has inexplicably "come unstuck in time". This is the poignant tale of a life-long romance between Henry, the time traveller, and Clare, the love of his life who is constantly left wondering when he will return next. Much of what makes this story so tragic is that it is completely rooted in Novikov's Self-Consistency Principle: even though Henry travels back and forth in time, he can never change anything about his past or future because everything is already carved in stone. What is about to happen has already happened, and will always have happened, and no matter how much we believe we have free will there is no way for us to change the path, even when we know where the path is headed. So, I have to admit a bit of a defeat on this one: much as I intellectually have to disagree with a story that is based upon there being only one timeline, which implies that our free will is just an illusion, there is no question that this is one of the most entrancing and moving novels I have come across in recent times. Clearly, for me this novel's "resonance" is based upon the depth of its characterizations, which allowed me to ignore the fact that I strongly disagree with the conclusions this book draws about the immutable nature of time.

Here's a completely shameless and self-serving proposition: "Imagining the Tenth Dimension" should be required reading for any writers planning on creating a story about time travel. The basic concepts from chapter one give a framework for how time can be manipulated, or moved within, and there are many ideas within the chapters that follow which could be excellent jumping off points for new fiction. Whether anyone chooses to play by these rules will, of course, be up to them (and Audrey Niffenegger would be an example of someone who probably would have chosen not to follow this book's line of reasoning even if she had been shown it). Nonetheless, there could well be moments within the telling of a new time travel story where this book's ideas could provide some useful input.

As we keep returning to, one of the main differences between the standard scientific view of reality and what we're exploring here begins with our explanation of the fourth dimension as being simultaneously both a spatial dimension and the dimension representing "duration", or time. Interestingly, this fascination with the possible nature of the fourth dimension is not as new as one might imagine. It became somewhat of a fad in the late 1800's and early 1900's, as evidenced by such literary works as H.G. Wells' "The Time Machine" (where a man travels through the fourth dimension to another time) and "The Invisible Man" (in which a man makes himself invisible by manipulating the fourth dimension), and William Faulkner's "As I Lay Dying" (in which the fourth dimension is presented as a vehicle for memory). The altered sense of space implied by the fourth dimension can be seen in the art of Duchamp and Picasso, and the photography of Muybridge. Even Salvador Dali's 1950 painting "Christus Hypercubus" (which depicts Christ being crucified on a fourth-dimensional hypercube, or "tesseract" as it is also known) demonstrates this same long-running fascination with the fourth dimension and what its true nature might be.

It should come as no surprise that the science fiction authors of more recent decades are the source of a cornucopia of delights when it comes to discussions of the nature of time and space. The gifted science fiction author Greg Bear wrote an excellent series of books ("Eon", "Eternity", and "Legacy") in which a privileged class of scientists acquires the ability to navigate through the worldlines that represent the alternate futures and pasts of our universe. Mr. Bear is blessed with the ability to write science fiction that incorporates enough hard science to make his suppositions feel very real, and the "theory of the universe" which he implies within his writing–in not just these particular novels but a number of his others as well–tends to be completely compatible with the multi-dimensional nature of reality as we are describing it here. I owe him a debt of gratitude for the ways which his writing has expanded my own concepts of how space, time and consciousness work together.

Likewise, Stephen Baxter's "Manifold" series of novels eloquently express the processes of repetition and exploration which are implied within these pages, and are useful in expanding one's concept of what our universe's different pasts and futures could contain. In particular, his descriptions of what the "end of the universe" could be like were influential in some of the ideas expressed in these pages.

It could be that there are other ways of navigating through higher dimensions that don't require us to invent a time machine. What if vivid dreams were actually our minds navigating through other fifth-dimensional realities as we sleep? What if dreams that had illogical/unpredictable jumps in them were because of sixth-dimensional "folds" that jumped us from one fifth-dimensional line to another? What if dreams of flying were actual memories of parts of our system of memes and beliefs (or, if you prefer, our soul) remembering what is it like to be free of our physical bodies and navigate through multi-dimensional time and space, free and unfettered?[xiv] We'll explore ideas such as this more in chapter nine.

EIGHT–DARK MATTER AND OTHER MYSTERIES

In 1919, a little-known mathematician, Theodor Kaluza sent a letter to Albert Einstein which left Mr. Einstein shocked and amazed. Einstein was so taken aback by what was proposed in Kaluza's article that it took him two years to respond, but when he did he recommended the letter be published in a respected scientific journal because of its significance. Kaluza's proposal was that the then current theories of gravity and light proposed by Einstein and Maxwell could be united if their field equations were calculated in the fifth rather than the fourth dimension. Kaluza's theories went on to be refined in 1926 by Oskar Klein, and during the twentieth century the resulting Kaluza-Klein theory went into, then out of, then back into favour, eventually becoming an important cornerstone of string theory.

This means that Kaluza's concept–that certain basic aspects of our reality are defined at the fifth dimension–has been an important consideration in physics for almost a century. For some reason though, this fact has failed to find its way into the consciousness of the general public. In the reality we are imagining in this book, the fifth dimension is also a cut-off point, because the sixth dimension contains the list of "you can't get there from here" points that will be inaccessible to us until someone perfects two-way time travel or wormhole technology.

When Kaluza wrote his groundbreaking letter to Einstein, the five dimensions he was using in his calculations were actually four spatial dimensions, and the fifth was time. Once again, what we are proposing here is that we reject as arbitrary the distinction of time being different from the other dimensions (as we discussed more fully in the chapter "The Flow of Time"). If we can accept time as just another spatial dimension this will be our jumping off point for discussing the following mysteries.

String theory tells us that the strength of gravity–like other physical constants–is defined by the harmonics (or "nodes", as they are also called) of superstrings vibrating in the tenth dimension. Physicists tell us that gravitational forces continue to exist in the higher dimensions above the four we live in.

Meanwhile, modern science has been wrestling for some time now with a quandary. The red-shifted light we see coming from distant stars is just like the doppler-shifted sound of a car horn, which has a higher pitch as it approaches us, and a lower pitch as it recedes into the distance. This shift towards the lower-frequency red wave-lengths we see in the light from distant stars tells us that those stars are moving away from us. Since this appears to be happening no matter what direction we look in the sky, this shows us that the universe is expanding, and it would appear to have been doing so since the big bang.

As we have discussed before, we find ourselves to be living in a "lucky" universe, where the initial big bang conditions created just the right balance between mass and the value of the gravitational force to create a universe which did not immediately collapse in upon itself, or did not immediately fly apart without allowing any significant matter to coalesce. So, by calculating the known mass and density of the universe, we should be able to see that the resulting gravitational attraction of all the stars, galaxies, nebulae, and so on to each other is someplace around the number that would be needed to have kept the universe from flying apart into virtual nothingness.

The quandary is this: when these numbers are calculated, scientists have come up with values that are far, far, below the mass that they would expect to have found based upon the observed speed of the universe's expansion. It turns out that as much as 90% of the mass of the universe must be made up of "missing matter" (this estimated number varies somewhat depending upon which theorist you consult and when in the last two decades you consulted them). In order to reconcile this, theorists have proposed that the missing mass is something called "dark matter". Dark matter is somehow completely invisible to us, but its mass would be what has exerted the gravitational pull on the stars and galaxies of the visible universe, which has kept the universe from flying apart into a formless void. Needless to say, the idea that nine tenths of the mass of our universe is made out of something which is invisible and undetectable is a very large mystery indeed.

If gravity exists in the fourth dimension and above (which is the current belief of string theorists), doesn't that mean our new way of viewing the ten dimensions offers a much simpler explanation of dark matter? If all other possible timelines do really exist, then isn't it conceivable that there will be a certain amount of gravitational pull from the fifth dimensional paths that are most adjacent to our current point in time, with the amount of "gravitational leakage" diminishing as we travel further away on a different fifth-dimensional path from our own fourth-dimensional line?

At any moment in the history of the universe, the number of future paths available to be chosen out of the quantum waves of indeterminacy will be the same. This is not to say that some paths won't take on substantially more significance for us as a species or for each of us as individuals, but rather that the sum of all available choices that are available will always be the same, which is why the "dark matter" gravitational pull our universe experiences does not constantly fluctuate up and down.

Plus, as we've already discussed, Feynman's "sum over paths" concept tells us that there are an equally large number of paths which could have been taken to arrive at the current moment, even though each of us are aware of only one of those paths. This means that the picture we're now imagining has an equally large amount of "gravitational leakage" that would be coming from those paths as well. This concept helps us to imagine how the gravitational pull from those other dimensions is not just pulling us forward in time towards the many branches we could be about to take, but is also coming from all of the paths which could have been taken to get us to any particular moment on our fourth-dimensional line.

Luckily, because gravity is the weakest of the four basic forces of the universe[14] we do not get trapped in a gravitational gridlock by all those adjacent universe, and the amount of gravitational leakage from one universe to the

---

[14] The four basic forces of the universe, in order of strength are:

1. Gravity. Although it is by far the weakest of the four, its strength is integral to the survival of our universe. Without gravity, the sun would explode, planets would not follow their orbits, and we would all be flung into space. Physicists theorize that gravity is the result of the exchange of as yet unseen particles called gravitons.

2. Electromagnetism. The force behind magnetism, electricity, laser beams, radio, and light, the electromagnetic force is actually made of tiny particles called photons. We keep mentioning how weak the force of gravity is compared to the other forces: electromagnetism is stronger than gravity by a factor of 1036. This is how the seemingly insubstantial static electricity charge in a comb can pick up little pieces of paper, thereby overcoming the gravity from an entire planet.

3. The Weak Nuclear Force. This force is responsible for the radioactive decay of particles, which contributes to the heat at the center of the earth and the fusion that drives both the sun and nuclear reactors. It is based on the interaction of electrons and neutrinos, which are exchanging other particles, called W- and Z-bosons.

4. The Strong Nuclear Force. This is what keeps the nuclei of most atoms from flying apart. Without the strong nuclear force the atoms and molecules of the universe would instantly disintegrate. The strong nuclear force results from the exchange of particles called, amusingly enough, gluons.

Eight – Dark Matter and Other Mysteries

next is relatively small compared to the forces in our own three dimensional reality.

In my personal opinion, this is the most exciting confirmation that the ten dimensions as we are imagining them here could truly be connected to the structure of reality—in this context, dark matter has a simple explanation. All we have to do is accept that time is a spatial dimension rather than a quality that we overlay on the other dimensions.

Within the past ten years, it has been determined that the universe's expansion is starting to accelerate, so cosmologists now believe that in addition to there being a large amount of dark matter in the universe which has kept the universe from flying apart too quickly during its first seven billion years or so, there is an even larger amount of "dark energy" which, during the universe's second seven billion years, is now starting to push the universe apart at a gradually increasing rate. This energy, like the dark matter we have just discussed, does not seem to be a part of our three dimensional space or our fourth dimensional time, it is somehow invisible even though its effect can be clearly seen. In order to explain this acceleration, a number of theories have been advanced, almost all of which imagine some sort of ubiquitous repulsive field which pervades our entire universe. The source of this repulsive Dark Energy force is still very much up for discussion in the world of physics.

Keeping in mind that the equation $E=mc^2$ defines an equivalent relationship between mass and energy, we would say that no matter what the actual total of all of the energy and mass within the universe is, it must equal 100% (we say this because if the number we arrived at didn't total 100%, then logically we would not be looking at all of the mass and energy). Based upon new observations, the current thinking is that the mass of our observed universe represents only 4% of what is really out there, while 23% of the universe is the dark matter we just described, whose mass has kept the universe from flying apart too quickly during the first 7 billion years of the universe. Amazingly, this means that the remaining 73% of the universe is this mysterious dark energy.[15]

According to string theory, the basic forces other than gravity do not affect the dimensions above ours. But as we surmised with dark matter, it is easy to imagine from our multi-dimensional viewpoint that this "dark energy" is somehow leaking into our reality from a higher dimension and pushing the universe apart. This force could well have always been there since the beginning of time, but it is only gaining the upper hand now that the universe is more expanded and mutual gravitational attraction is less of a factor. As with dark matter, we can imagine that this energy is being summed from the many adjacent fifth dimensional universes which are "just around the corner", which is why we cannot see its source from our current dimensional viewpoint. Could we be seeing a repulsive force introduced by the fact that the nearby particles in those adjacent universes have the same charge as the ones in ours, so their like polarity is driving each other apart just as two magnets placed north pole to north pole would? While this theory may seem tempting, it's hard to ignore that physicists tell us that the forces other than gravity do not exert themselves into the higher dimensions.

---

[15] Hold on, now we're saying that 23% of the universe is dark matter. But didn't we just say a few paragraphs ago that as much as 90% of the mass of the universe is missing? Let's back up and do some math. According to modern science, the total mass of the universe (mass being the component whose gravity draws the universe together) represents only 27% of what's really out there, while the remaining part is dark energy. But out of that 27%, only 4% is visible, while the rest is dark matter. Four divided by twenty-seven is 15% so that would indeed mean that 85% of the universe's total mass is somehow invisible.

And it means that an astonishing 73% represents the unexplained dark energy which now appears to be causing the universe to gradually accelerate its expansion during its second 7 billion years. While the very specific numbers quoted continue to fluctuate somewhat depending upon which expert you consult, the general consensus in the physics community remains that our universe and the particles from which we currently believe it to be constructed represent only a tiny portion of what must really be out there. Considered together, dark matter and dark energy remain one of the biggest and most challenging mysteries of modern science.

Eight – Dark Matter and Other Mysteries

So, if gravity is the only one of the four basic forces that is supposed to travel across higher dimensions, is there any other way we can explain this mysterious repulsive force which is currently driving the universe apart at an ever-increasing rate?

One possible explanation could be that what we are witnessing is not a repulsive force at all, but an attractive one. Here is a possibility that was first advanced by physicist Paul Steinhardt: you may recall the "Big Splat" theory which we touched on before, which suggested that every trillion years or so two adjacent branes (the one which parts of the superstrings creating our universe are embedded within, and another one containing the superstrings of another universe) are drawn to each other by mutual gravitational attraction, accelerating and then colliding together, creating two new big bang universes. So, as disturbing as it might be to contemplate, what if the expansion of our current universe was already beginning to occur as the initial phase of our upcoming Big Splat? This would seem unlikely unless the estimate of "every trillion years" was way off, but it is difficult to imagine what it will be like to be on a brane which is beginning that long process of acceleration towards another brane.

This accelerated expansion might be easier for us to imagine if we also imagine that the brane we are being drawn to is much bigger than the brane we are currently on, so that the outside edges of our universe are being sucked out towards an even larger brane universe. From our vantage point, then, it would appear that our universe is being driven apart by this unexplained Dark Energy phenomenon, when in fact it is the gravity of another nearby brane universe which is pulling our universe apart. Does the adjacent universe actually have to be larger than ours for this observed outward acceleration to take place? Let's just say that this is a useful concept for helping us to imagine how this process could result in the expansion physicists have been observing. The boggling implications of what it would mean to have, for instance, another universe in the seventh dimension (or on a seventh-dimensional brane) exerting gravitational pull on our three-dimensional universe may be closer to the truth of what we are imagining here.

In a way, Dark Matter and Dark Energy could be thought of as very old concepts. The ancient Greeks proposed that the universe is infused with an "aether" which fills all of space because nature abhors a vacuum. In the 19th century it was widely believed that the entire universe contained a "luminiferous aether" which was the medium that carried light from one point to another. Einstein's theory of relativity appeared to prove that there was no such need for a luminiferous aether. And yet, ironically, Einstein then proposed the existence of a similarly all-pervasive force when his calculations from general relativity first showed that the universe could easily have had a compressed beginning and a continuing expansion thereafter. Einstein, like most of his contemporaries, simply "knew" that the universe was destined to be eternal and unchanging, not expanding, so therefore there had to be an error in his analysis. To correct this "error", in 1917 he introduced an arbitrary factor which he called the "cosmological constant". This clever addition to his equations could, depending upon the value it is set to, result in a universe that was either shrinking or expanding at any rate desired. Choosing one specific value for this constant allowed Einstein to produce equations that showed the universe to be stable, as he expected it to be. Ten years later, however, new evidence of red-shifted light from distant stars showed the universe really is expanding after all.

For the remainder of his life, Einstein called the cosmological constant his life's greatest mistake. And yet, since the death of Einstein, there have been numerous guises in which versions of his cosmological constant could be said to have reappeared, for instance in something called the "Higgs Ocean" and in a factor called "quintessence". Any of these might eventually be proved to be a part of what we currently know of as the dark energy which currently appears to be driving the universe apart.

In string theory, it is usually (but not always) supposed that the higher six dimensions above our four are curled up on themselves, and inconceivably tiny. How does that connect to the version of reality we are exploring here? Most likely it does not. The point of our discussion is to expand the mind, to allow the average non-scientist to find a way to imagine what ten spatial dimensions stacked on top of each other could be like–a mental achievement that most of us would have rejected as an impossibility. If, along the way, we come up with some useful insights that prove to be connected to the way the universe really turns out to function, then we really will have accomplished something here.

Consider this: the idea that the higher dimensions are invisible to us because they are curled up on themselves is, according to what we've constructed here, an unnecessary embellishment. If we can return again to our two-dimensional race of Flatlanders, let's imagine a Flatlander Physicist who has become convinced that reality is constructed from superstrings vibrating in the tenth dimension. To a Flatlander, "time" would be the third dimension, because it would be what they move through to get from one instant to another in their two-dimensional existence. As we discussed before, here in the third dimension we can make appointments by giving fourth-dimensional co-ordinates: "I'll meet you on the third floor of the building at the corner of Scarth Street and Eleventh Avenue at 4:30 this afternoon". For us, the first three co-ordinates describe a point in three-dimensional space, while the fourth co-ordinate provides a point in fourth-dimensional time. If a Flatlander were going to arrange to meet a friend somewhere, they would only have to supply three co-ordinates: the first two would be the X and Y values that intersect to define a position in their two-dimensional universe, and the third would be the time of the meeting.

Our Flatlander Physicist, believing that reality is created in the tenth dimension, would then have to come up with an explanation for why there was no way for him to observe those seven higher dimensions. For him, one explanation would be to theorize that it was his unique condition as a conscious creature living in the second dimension that made him unable to observe any dimensions higher than the third. Any attempts to perceive those higher dimensions is impossible for him–not because those dimensions are curled up into tiny coils down at the Planck length[16], but merely because his two-dimensional consciousness is collapsing reality at the second dimension into a third dimensional timeline. Nonetheless, an explanation that involved the seven higher dimensions being curled up on themselves might be the conclusion that our Flatlander Physicist could arrive at as well.

As we've discussed before, the same would be true for any creature or consciousness that you could imagine existing in any dimension: "time" will, for each of them, always be the next dimension up. We have also already argued that perceiving the tenth dimension as a whole is impossible: in chapter ten, we'll touch on a theory which could explain how this can be.

Here's an important corollary to this way of thinking: if the next dimension above (no matter what dimension a form of consciousness might exist within) is always "time", then the dimensions below are always just geometry that we are navigating through. This is important because it helps us to understand why omnipotent beings living in the highest dimensions haven't used their god-like powers to crush us all: for them, this would be an impossibility. Think about this for a moment: we have already imagined that if we were to simultaneously perceive all possible beginnings and endings and all possible timelines for the universe we live in, this would be nothing more than a point in the seventh dimension. To a creature in the ninth dimension, then, all the actions, dreams, motivations and desires that any of we human beings down here in the third and fourth dimension

---

[16] We'll discuss Max Planck's "Planck length" and "Planck time" more in chapter ten.

Eight – Dark Matter and Other Mysteries

might be feeling would be not only invisible to them, but inconceivable. To that creature, the sum total of our universe's futures and pasts would just be a single point that they navigate through, and by navigating through that point they would be able to move to another point which is unrelated to our own universe. In other words, passing through the point that represents our infinity of timelines would just be that, passing through, and it would be impossible for a creature from that higher dimension to have any direct effect on that point.

Likewise, if we imagine a one-dimensional line, and choose a point on that line, then that point can be perceived by us from the third dimension. Let's say that specific point on that imaginary one-dimensional line is now floating in front or your face. From our third dimensional perspective, that one-dimensional co-ordinate will never change. We can move to that point, we can move through that point, but no matter what we do, that point will always be where it is, by its very definition. Anything that we perceive of as *changing* that point is actually happening as a result of interactions in higher dimensions than the first. In other words, I can pass my hand through that point in front of me, I can blow that point up with an atom bomb, but in the first dimension that point will still be that point, by its very definition: it's "just geometry".

In the same sense, the fourth dimensional point you are experiencing at this instant as you read these words will always be that point, and anything that happens a second later is a different fourth dimensional point, equally unchangeable. In other parts of this text we have imagined ways that we can move through these fourth dimensional points as we select them from possible branches in the fifth dimension, but from the fifth dimension, each of those fourth dimensional instants are "just geometry": they are just points that you can pass through, but passing through

Eight – Dark Matter and Other Mysteries

them cannot change them, any more than you can change that point one foot in front of your face.[17]

Another way of thinking about this idea takes us back to chapter one, where we imagined what we three-dimensional creatures would look like to a two-dimensional Flatlander. To the Flatlander, our bodies would be seen in cross-section only—a hand entering their world might start out as four lines (which would be the flat cross-section discs of the fingers as seen from the flat plane of the Flatlander), soon joined by a fifth shape (the thumb), and those five shapes would soon merge into a larger shape (a cross-section of a hand). It would seem that we three-dimensional creatures would have god-like powers in the second dimension, with the ability to pop in and out of existence and mutate through inexplicable forms.

We've imagined this from the perspective of the Flatlanders, but now let's imagine it from our own three-dimensional viewpoint. Because the Flatlanders are in the immediately adjacent dimension to our own three-dimensional space, it's easier for us to imagine that we could somehow have an effect on their world. It might seem that being able to pop in and out of existence should at least allow us to blunder around and effect some destruction, much like a bull in a China Shop. But since we cannot actually narrow our perceptions down to two dimensions, how would we actually be able to effect any meaningful change? In other words, how would we communicate and interact with a Flatlander?

The answer is simple. If I were to become a Flatlander, somehow limiting my awareness down to their perception of lines and shapes that are nearer and farther to them within their flat two-dimensional plane of existence, I would become a quantum observer who was collapsing a three-dimensional timeline into a second-dimensional

---

[17] To be clear about this, we are not arguing here for the existence of pre-destination: it's important to remember that our free will allows us to choose from the available branches any of the next available points as we move along our fourth-dimensional line. We will discuss this idea more in a few pages.

Eight – Dark Matter and Other Mysteries

world, and I would be able to interact with and effect changes down there. Human myths and religions are rife with such stories: a god or god-like creature takes on human form. By becoming human, in some mythologies they may also become subject to the limitations of our human world, and can even end up dying: but by entering our dimension they can have significant impact which would have been impossible had they stayed in their own much higher plane of existence.

Finally, even if we were to imagine omnipotent higher-dimensional beings who wanted to "use their godlike powers to crush us all", we end up with the often-maligned anthropic viewpoint which we have already used to explain the constant string of doomsayers predicting the end of the world. Let's say there are timelines where those doomsayers were right. That would mean there was a timeline where the end of the world happened, and there is no one left here to have this discussion. So, even if we can think a way for the higher-dimensional-creatures-crushing-us-all timeline to have occurred, we know that is not the timeline we are on, so it has no relevance to our world.

In chapter three we imagined a scenario with a reverse-time alien race who arrived here five seconds ago, and (on their reverse timeline) went on to wipe out the human race in what we think of as our past. At that point in the text we argued that if those aliens had succeeded in their mission, it would make no difference to us, because in the timeline we are experiencing we are clearly aware that it did not happen. This is a daunting concept–like the famous science fiction paradox we looked at in chapter seven, where someone goes back in time, kills their grandfather, and therefore doesn't exist because they were never born, the difficulties of imagining such loops in time without getting caught in sticky contradictions are many indeed.

A worldview that imagines these different scenarios as "just geometry" leads us to a way out. So, we know the line we are on does not have genocidal reverse-time aliens arriving five seconds ago, because if that line were the one we are now on our forebears would have been destroyed and we would not be here to comment. That is not to say that there isn't some other timeline where this unfortunate event occurred: but if we think of time being a geometrical construct, we can see how the apparent paradoxes of such scenarios can be resolved.

Before we leave the little tangent we're on here, let's review some of the concepts we have explored elsewhere which tie into our current discussion. The idea of the moment you are experiencing at this instant as being "just geometry" means, as we have discussed before, that there are multiple paths which could have caused you to arrive at this particular moment, and the path that you remember as being your personal history is only one of many which could have brought you to this present moment in time (as you will recall from the discussion of Feynman's "sum over paths" theory which we first looked at in chapter four). The image of the extraordinarily extravagant multiverse that is inferred from this concept is something we discussed in the Introduction, as this ties directly to Everett's "Many Worlds Theory" and "decoherence", both of which have been enjoying renewed support in the last few years. And finally, we should always be mindful of the double-edged sword that is implied by the idea of the current instant of time being "just geometry": while this means that the potential for this instant of time has always existed within the tenth dimension (as have all the potential moments to come and all the ones that could have already occurred), it does not mean that our path is somehow carved in stone and unavoidable. As creatures with free will, we are constantly moving through the fifth dimensional paths that are available to us, selecting one of those paths as our personal timeline. The path that we have been on makes the next possible choice the more likely one (and that would be the one predicted by the sum over paths method), but a life-changing decision or event that breaks old habits and old patterns will certainly direct a person's life to a new trajectory, making other future paths more likely to be followed from that point on. Of course, this also means that a life-changing negative event, whether it is self-directed or the result of some external circumstance, will also place a person's world-line on a new trajectory, and make other paths that had been available either much less likely, or even impossible from that moment on. [xv]

The "Power of No" should never be underestimated. Any time a connection fails to be made, or an acquaintance is ignored, or an opportunity is not taken, potential fifth dimensional paths are being closed off. Discussions of "free will" often focus on the paths that a person deliberately takes, but paths that are not taken due to choice, or indifference, or ignorance have effects that can be just as far-reaching in a person's life.

So, for us, the fourth dimension is time, and any instant that we look at from our current timeline is actually just a "point" in the geometry of all possible third dimensional realities which our universe could potentially contain. No matter what dimension we exist in, then, our perception of the dimension above the one we are physically in as "time" will give us the illusion of that dimension being more limited than the full spatial dimension that it really is, and the "arrow of time" will make us believe that dimension can only be one single line. Isn't it true, though, that there are indications each of us see that time connects to itself in various other non-linear ways? Does our personal perception of time not vary according to many factors?

As we discussed in chapter five, it is not unusual for us to have the perception that time is more than an inexorable ticking timekeeper which marches forward every second, and there are times when our awareness of the passage of time is quite distorted.

Time is also a medium which connects things and allows information to be transferred through itself. For instance, how does a newborn babe know how to suckle? How are birds who have never migrated before able to navigate huge distances to specific locations? How is it that certain sounds

Eight – Dark Matter and Other Mysteries

like the scrape of chalk on a chalkboard are almost universally reviled? These are all examples of information which has somehow been encoded into our existence to be carried across time. Instinct, racial memory, and innate behaviours are, like the memes and belief systems we discussed in chapter five, systems that connect through the fourth, fifth and sixth dimension to allow information to be communicated and preserved across time. Some strands of DNA have instructions in them that may not need to be decoded for tens of thousands of years, but then a specific circumstance will arise and that information will become available when it is needed. These are all examples of systems which exist across time, folding it in various ways just as we would crumple a piece of paper, allowing one part and then another to make contact with each other.

Instantaneous connections that we see every day are also indications that time is a medium which can be navigated within, not just as an arrow relentlessly moving forward. Fascinating books such as Tompkins and Bird's "The Secret Life of Plants" (in which it is demonstrated that plants are much more aware of their surroundings than we might imagine) and Rupert Sheldrake's "Dogs That Know When Their Masters are Coming Home: and Other Unexplained Powers of Animals" (which documents such mysterious phenomena as animals being aware of coming natural disasters which scientists have not been able to predict)[18] present us with documentation of what is already apparent to most human beings–that the natural world is connected together in ways that transcend the limitations of speech and touch, allowing instantaneous communication of information to lifeforms that are open enough to receive it. The movie "What the Bleep Do We Know" tells us of a Japanese experimenter who has even extended this research to water molecules, coming up with seemingly outlandish proofs that seem to indicate an ability for water to respond to emotion. Many experts would, of course, dismiss

---

[18] Sheldrake coined the term "morphic resonance" to describe this effect of information and emotion being transmitted through unseen channels across space and time.

Eight – Dark Matter and Other Mysteries

examples such as these as "crackpot theories", or perhaps they would assign them the slightly less derogatory label of "fringe science".

Terms like "fringe science" will usually make mainstream scientists turn on their blinders. Anything that can be categorized under this label, they would say, is obviously not worthy of any serious research or consideration. Brian Josephson is a famous example of a respected scientist who has been forced to forsake his established position within the mainstream world of physics because of his desire to see more rigorous scientific methods applied to certain kinds of "fringe science".

Brian is a Nobel Laureate whose "Josephson Junctions" began as a theory which sprang from his profound understanding of superconductivity and quantum tunnelling. These Josephson Junctions have become one of the most powerful tools currently being used for research into the subtle magnetic fields of the brain, of earthquake prediction, and of the gravity waves predicted by modern cosmologists' theories of the beginning of the universe. His innovative discoveries certainly qualify him as one of the great minds of the twentieth century.

However, somewhat unexpectedly, Mr. Josephson is now a famous advocate for research into the physics behind paranormal phenomena. Here's what he says on his website (www.tcm.phy.cam.ac.uk/~bdj10/): "One of my guiding principles ... has been the scientist's motto 'Take nobody's word for it' (*nullius in verba*), a corollary of which is that if scientists as a whole denounce an idea this should not necessarily be taken as proof that the said idea is absurd: rather, one should examine carefully the alleged grounds for such opinions and judge how well these stand up to detailed scrutiny". Mr. Josephson also documents on his website some of the efforts he feels the established scientific community has made to ridicule and discredit any research which falls outside the commonly accepted norms, which would certainly include Mr. Josephson's research into the physics of the paranormal.

Eight – Dark Matter and Other Mysteries

Regardless of the position that mainstream science takes on the topic, a huge percentage of the general population have had personal experiences which show them that the idea of reading minds, "catching vibes", supernatural connections to dead loved ones, or even just the positive effects of talking to their houseplants has a direct connection to their feeling of how the world really works. These are all examples of how time can be navigated laterally to exchange information, not just as a single straight line.

All of the body's senses have ways to connect through our minds and our memories to other points in time and space. Sights, sounds, smells, and even textures can conjure up connections that are part of the complex system of memes that make up our individual experience across the higher spatial dimensions we are now imagining as being used to construct the ten dimensions of reality.[xvi]

How about the well-known experience of a certain smell vividly bringing to mind a moment from the past? Scents and pheremones are known to be powerfully and intricately tied to memory and instinct, in ways that would seem to fold time. Could molecules of a certain scent that brings to mind a certain memory be exerting their power in part because those molecules are clumped together in a higher dimension? If that were the case, the doorway to the memes and memories of a different time and place could be much more easily accessed when the same fragrance is encountered again, because in a higher dimension that different time and place really would be in that much closer proximity to each other.

Sounds also can trigger memory and even instinct. We have already mentioned the squealing sound of chalk on a chalkboard being commonly reviled. Could this because it resembles the cry of some prehistoric predator which our distant ancestors learned that they should retreat from as quickly as possible? Or, as another example, could the desire to urinate at the sound of running water be a racial memory that connects us to our ancestors who chose to urinate in a place where their urine would be carried away? That would mean the potential ancestors we could have had who constantly chose to urinate in their own standing drinking water supply died of disease, did not become our ancestors, and therefore we have no connection across time to them. As we discussed before, these ideas can also tie into the work of Richard Dawkins, who proposed a new way of looking at genes and how their "desire for continuance" connects them from the past to today in a "river out of Eden".

Water is particularly interesting when considered as a medium across time, since we as human beings are mostly water. Do you recall imagining ourselves four-dimensionally, as a snakelike creature with the embryonic self at one end and the dead self at the other? Now imagine the water that we are mostly made up of in four-dimensional terms. Obviously, some of the water that is in us now is not the water that was in us a week ago, as there is a constant depletion and replenishment taking place (by the way, keep in mind that we're not just talking about urination here: water leaves our bodies as vapour in our breath, as perspiration, as evaporation). Parts of the water that was in us today could have been in someone else last month, or up in the sky, or inside a plant, or in a reservoir, and so on. Imagining the interconnected fourth- and fifth-dimensional paths of water that flow in and out of each of us creates a gloriously interconnected web that surrounds the earth. What if it were really true that water molecules are able to respond to emotion and carry information? Here is an internet that our current world of technology can only dream of.

The same is true of all the molecules in our bodies. We are constantly going through a process of exchange and renewal, so that in the passing of ten years many of the molecules inside our body are not the same as the ones that were there previously. Imagine the fourth- and fifth-dimensional net connecting the carbon that was in your body ten years ago with where it is today. Imagine the connections across time and space back to the creation of that carbon in the dying of other stars billions of years ago, since that is where all carbon in our universe comes from originally. Once again, the image of a fantastically huge new web of connections is made, and those connections are invisible and unknown to us within our limited viewpoint travelling along our narrow fourth-dimensional line.[xvii]

As quantum observers, unseen connections would be our standard mode of operation. One of the implications we have not discussed so far is how the process of choosing which of the possible realities available to us at a given moment might work. Is the brain, invisible to our conscious mind, actually able to process the multiple strands available to us and choose the one that is most preferred at a given moment? This would be a huge amount of processing for us to be doing, but not particularly different from the massive processing of sensory information we know the brain is already doing. Receiving, categorizing, and interpreting this astonishing range of input data–in a process that is essentially transparent to our conscious mind–is what the brain does already. So, in that sense, if there is a part of us that is able to sense the fifth dimensional pathways currently available to us and pick one over another, this may not be that much of a leap over the processing that is already occurring.

To be clear though, what we are talking about is a different process from the conscious act of deciding "what should I do next", even though the two processes may be intricately entwined. What we are suggesting is that, in our role as quantum observers, there could be a part of us which is actually able to peer into the near-future outcomes that could be available to us within the quantum wave function, and steer our course towards the path we are more interested in taking. Julian Jaynes' Bicameral Mind theory comes to mind again: as he described it, a previous mode of operation for all human beings in millennia gone by would have been to hear such input as the voice of the Gods or a departed relative. Perhaps we as modern humans still hear the input of our quantum observer, but nowadays this might manifest itself as intuition, judgement, our gut reaction, guidance from above, "just a feeling", or similar mental processes such as this. In extreme cases, this would be clairvoyance, prescience, spirit visions, and other capabilities generally categorized as being supernatural.

Each of us has unique ways of processing the incoming information from our senses that would make it very difficult to drop into someone else's mind. Marvin Minsky's "Society of Mind" shows how many small processes can be linked together in hierarchies and feedback loops to create what we think of as "the mind". These processes start in the womb and become increasingly multi-layered and intricate as we approach adulthood. But there are many, many ways to achieve that network of mental processes that becomes a functioning individual.

A common fallacy, then, is to presume that everyone sees and hears the same way you do. The fact is, each person has different ways of processing the data that is entering through their senses. What would it be like to drop into the mind of the velociraptors we saw in the film Jurassic Park who (according to the movie) could only see things that are moving? The science fiction idea of dropping into someone else's mind or trying to download someone else's memories (ideas explored a number of times in the writing of Philip K. Dick) could be just as alien as trying to enter the mind of a 'raptor. For instance, some humans have a great deal more difficulty processing foreground sounds if there are too many simultaneous background sounds. Others will focus to the point where they may not even be aware that other sound sources (or echoes of the foreground sounds from surrounding reflective surfaces) are there. Some people experience a condition called synaesthesia, where their senses are mixed in surprising ways: they taste textures, or they see sounds, for instance. Many of us feel that memory and smell are intricately tied together, but where does this leave someone whose sense of smell has never been strong?

Each of us have different ways of experiencing the world, of remembering a past event, and organizing that information for future triggering and future use. As we'll explore in the next few pages, there are other reasons why suddenly dropping one's consciousness into someone else's body could be not just disorienting, but a completely overwhelming and perhaps even dangerously painful experience.

Have you ever sat in a room with a tape recorder and made a recording, then listened back and been surprised at how much background noise there was? Part of the reason this occurs–purely apart from bad electronics or a cheap microphone–is because of the way the brain processes and rejects extraneous data. Here is a useful saying in discussions of life and consciousness: "that which ceases to change ceases to exist". When the brain processes input from the auditory nerve, it tends to reject any continuous noises which do not change–like, for instance, the noise of the air molecules in the room banging into each other, or the sound of an air conditioner. In other words, for our consciousness, the noises (or smells, or continuous aches and pains, and so on) which cease to change, will cease to exist because the brain stops them from being considered for processing. When we listen back to the tape recording, we are hearing what's really in the room, without the phase reversed noise cancellation the brain uses to remove those continuous noises. Now, when the internal mechanisms of the ear are damaged, usually through exposure to excessive sound levels, we end up with an imbalance, where the brain is correcting for frequencies that are no longer coming in. This manifests itself as tinnitus, or "ringing of the ears". It turns out that the ringing we hear is not from the ears, but from the brain itself, as it attempts to cancel out particular frequencies that are no longer coming in from the auditory nerve.

This is an example of how the brain is processing a huge amount of data, while our conscious minds are completely unaware of the process. It is only when things are not functioning normally that we start to see evidence of what's going on "behind the curtain". There are other well-known side effects and artifacts when the brain is not correctly processing the real-time data that we know it is dealing with every minute. "The Man Who Mistook His Wife for a Hat", by Oliver Sacks, contains fascinating examples of some of the more exotic results of neurological impairment.

Almost everyone is familiar with the experience of entering an environment with a strong smell which seems almost overpowering, and yet shortly thereafter we cease to notice it. For our olfactory glands, "that which ceases to change ceases to exist" is definitely the normal mode of operation. So, ten minutes after entering a space that has a strong aroma, we are often no longer aware of it. This is not because the entire olfactory system has shut down though, as many of us are then able to pick out much more subtle scents like the perfume, tobacco smoke, or food smells that are attached to a new person entering that same environment.

Each of us are processing and rejecting a unique pattern of repetitive inputs from our physical bodies, our senses, and our own internal thought processes. The "indomitable human spirit" that allows some of us to continue in circumstances that others would perceive as being completely impossible to contend with can be a noble thing. But this is also one of the dangerous pitfalls of human existence: a person can become so accustomed to a way of living that others would find intolerable that they never attempt to find a way out. If there is really no other way for that person to exist, then their acceptance of their situation can be an inspiration to us all. If there is a way out but the person's mind has ceased to notice there is even a problem, then we see another sad story of a wasted life in the making.

"That which ceases to change ceases to exist" also applies nicely to the ten dimensions as we have imagined them here. If it is superstrings vibrating in the tenth dimension that create the world we see around us, when they cease to vibrate then we cease to exist. As we discussed back in chapter three, this process is really tied to our role as quantum observers. By observing a certain reality, we are collapsing out what the results of certain superstring vibrations would have been had they been vibrating, and

Eight – Dark Matter and Other Mysteries

effectively this is exactly the same thing as observing the reality that results from the vibrations of strings in the tenth dimension. Nothing ever really happens in the tenth dimension, because as soon as anything "tries to", it immediately collapses out a reality in the dimensions below which we, as quantum observers, are witness to.

What would it feel like to have the brain not efficiently processing the quantum data that we are suggesting it is also having to deal with? Could it be that the loss of peripheral vision that happens when people are tired or sick is a function of the brain looking down the long tunnel of coming quantum timelines and not having time to provide all of the visual data currently coming in? Could the experience of an ocular migraine–where the vision becomes overlaid with fast-rotating little dots and circles, or fluttering vibrations (often triggered by stress or overwork)– actually be a glimpse into this behind-the-scenes processing of quantum indeterminacy that the brain is doing?[xviii]

There are drugs which seers and mystics have used to trigger visions which they claimed showed them the secrets of the universe. Could such drugs as peyote or LSD offer ways of opening doors into the quantum nature of reality, revealing the fluid nature of time to those who partake? And systematic derangement of the senses as a pathway to enlightenment need not be drug-induced either: chanting, drumbeats, meditation, exercise, and many other repetitive actions are often touted as a way for the seeker to find a different plane. Could that plane be outside of our limited fourth dimension?

There are also perceptual effects that some people describe as having occurred only the first time they ingest a particular drug or go through a particular first experience. Could the minor hallucinations some people experience with their first marijuana high be a glimpse of the swirling eddies that represent their near-future realities spinning off from their current moment, reminiscent of the shapes on a three-dimensional paisley fabric? Could the spots before the eyes and light-headedness of the "first cigarette" that some people describe, and which they then spend decades trying and failing to re-create be more than just a side effect of lowered oxygen supply to the brain, and actually be a perception of their possible futures that are now being cut off by their decision to smoke? Could part of the exhilaration and heightened sense of their surroundings that some persons experience the first time they successfully achieve a particular physical task be because of their connection to new physical futures that are now possible for them because of their reaching this particular milestone?

Meditation is a particularly interesting example of how people can use the power of the mind to change their health and circumstances. Researchers analyzing the EEGs of persons in a meditative state have seen that the parietal lobe, which processes incoming data to give a person the sense of their location in time and space, becomes much less active during meditation. If the parietal lobe would be what anchors us in the first-through-fourth dimension (time and space), then, could suppressing that part of the brain be what opens the person who is meditating up to the healing paths available to them in higher dimensions? This leads us to our next chapter.

Eight – Dark Matter and Other Mysteries

NINE-HOW MUCH CONTROL DO WE HAVE?

Have you ever met someone who claimed they had been too busy to get a cold, so they continued working and stayed healthy? Perhaps that person also mentioned that after a month or two they took a break and suddenly the cold sent them to bed. What is the mechanism that could allow a body to avoid or at least stave off a virus for so long, while others nearby are immediately struck down with the same virus? Could this be an example of people finding a way to collapse a different quantum reality simply through their desire to do so?

There have been examples of cancer patients who have successfully used creative visualization to imagine their body's defences attacking a tumour, rendering themselves cancer-free without surgery. Could these people have found a way, through their own strength of will, to navigate to a different fifth-dimensional timeline?

The movie "What the Bleep Do We Know" strongly takes the position that we are all quantum observers creating our own reality. It describes a 1993 experiment in Washington

D.C. where a group of spiritualists all concentrated through transcendental meditation on lowering the crime rate for a summer. Police officials and sociologists were stunned to see that violent crime fell some 23% below its usual levels that summer (a more detailed analysis of this study can be viewed at http://www.istpp.org/crime_prevention/). Is this an example of enough people being able to bend our reality to meet a desired end simply through concentrating on their desire for it to happen? (Some naysayers suggest this is more of an example of how statistics can be manipulated to a desired interpretation: it would be a shame if that's true because this experiment makes such a great story!)

People who pray for the health of another, or who promise to send "positive vibes" towards their fellow human beings could really be exacting change through their role as quantum observers.[xix] All of us are both transmitters and receivers for these vibrations, though clearly some of us have much stronger capacities in one ability over the other. In physics, this process is known as "entrainment", where vibrations from one source can cause other vibrating entities to fall into step with them.[19] Charismatic speakers who can

---

[19] This effect was first noted in 1665 by Dutch scientist Christian Huygens, who (amongst numerous other innovations) invented the pendulum clock. He made the surprising discovery that his clocks tend to fall into exact synchrony when placed close to each other. The effect disappears if the clocks are at right angles to each other or are separated by more than six feet. He found that when they are side by side, within an hour or so the pendulums will have begun to swing in exact opposition to each other, like two hands clapping, and will tend to stay in sync thereafter. After some mystification, Huygens proved that this mysterious effect was the result of tiny vibrations being communicated from one clock to the other through the wood beams the clocks were hanging from, or the surface the clocks were sitting on.

Entrainment is used in "brain machines" which use flashing lights and/or rhythmic sound to influence brainwave patterns: the process of entrainment will cause the subject's brainwave patterns to be influenced, drawing the mind into states that are more desired. Entrainment of brain waves is not always a desired effect though. One of the most famous examples of entrainment with negative results occurred in Japan on December 16 1997, when a particularly extreme sequence of flashing visual effects in an episode of the cartoon series "Pokemon" triggered seizures in children across the country, sending 600 to the hospital. The impact of the effect was probably heightened by the Japanese culture's tendency towards smaller rooms and larger televisions, so when the flashing effects occurred a substantial portion of a stricken child's field of vision was probably filled, causing the disruption of brainwave patterns into undesired patterns to be that much more intense.

Nine – How Much Control Do We Have?

sway a room with their words are clearly transmitting something strong which we could say bends the consensual reality of that group towards a new fifth-dimensional path. And some people are able to transmit feelings and auras without saying a word, whether that be good or bad. Have you found that just being in the same room as a certain person makes you feel edgy, or depressed? Perhaps, then, you are a person who is more of a receiver than a transmitter, and therefore the spiritual vibrations of others are more likely to affect you. Some strongly gifted receivers use their empathetic skills to become doctors, health care professionals, even psychics or healers. Some of these concepts are explored in the previously mentioned Steven Strogatz book "Sync".

Love and hate, then, are extreme examples of these vibrations. The loving support of a spouse, a parent, a family member, or a friend really can have an influence on which fifth dimensional line is collapsed into our fourth-dimensional reality. Likewise, hate can have a powerful negative influence on the path of someone else's life. If that's the case, then why can't someone "kill with a look"? Perhaps someone could, but this is usually impossible to achieve because there are many balancing forces at any one moment that tend to cancel out the most extreme impulses, as we'll discuss more later in this chapter.

If we were each to analyze the fourth dimensional timeline of our lives so far, most of us would probably categorize certain days as good/bad, happy/sad, productive/wasteful, and so on. We might be able to generalize these categorizations down to weeks, months, or even years. Recalling how we have seen that it's possible to be moving in higher dimensions and be unaware of that movement in the dimension below, what if we were to now plot our life's analysis on an x/y graph, with the passage of time represented as a straight line from left to right, and a squiggly line moving from left to right above and below that straight line representing the positive and negative categorizations we applied to the different parts of our life? In a simple sense, we are now plotting the fifth dimensional path (or "world-line") that represents what we think of as the fourth dimensional line of our lives so far. How much of your life is above the line, how much below?[xx] Would you like the rest of your life-line to have a different shape than the one you've drawn so far?[xxi]

Psychoactive substances that create the illusion of being "above the line" can also give people a fun ride for a while, but the short-term problems of hangovers and next-day depression which can lead to long-term problems of dependency, addiction and major damage to health make such substances very dangerous. In other words, an artificial high introduced by alcohol or other drugs that gives people the feeling that their personal timeline is riding above that midpoint line is likely to have a rebound effect that will be put people "below the line" when they are not relying on the effect of those substances, and the long-term damage to health caused by those substances means they will eventually be responsible for a life that constantly remains "below the line". By that point, some people still remain trapped in the same cycle, and the commonly heard phrase is "I just have to take the stuff to feel normal".[20] In other words, the person has reduced their general vitality to the point where what used to give them the feeling of being "above the line" functions now only to push them back to some place near their midpoint.

Getting back to the concept of transmitters and receivers, we can see how some people can, even without their knowledge, have a negative or positive effect on others, purely by how much above or below the line their lives would be represented on the graph we have just imagined. As we navigate through the countless possibilities of the fifth dimension, each of us has the potential to change our own path, or to have our path changed by others. One might say that actions that result in the continuance of life are good, and actions that result in death are bad, but it is easy to come up with examples where the death of a murderous

---

[20] Or "I just have to drink / smoke / shoot / snort / eat …" we can insert whatever the preferred mode of ingestion might be for any particular vice.

Nine – How Much Control Do We Have?

psychopath is a good rather than a bad thing. One could choose to say that actions that result in the continuance of the universe are good, and actions that result in the eventual end of the universe are bad, but being able to determine which events will have which outcome is virtually impossible when we try to make those evaluations from our limited fourth dimensional window. And clearly, the question of right and wrong is sometimes just a question of point of view, as many centuries of religious conflict have shown us.

When we discuss big picture concepts such as "actions that result in the eventual end of the universe", some would suggest that is impossible, because time is like a river. What do we mean by that? If we step out into a river and jam a big stick into the riverbed, we will create some minor turbulence that might last for a few feet, but the overall path of the river will remain unchanged. Let's say instead that we drop a gigantic boulder in the river, blocking off fully half of the river at that point. Although there might be some new flooding in the immediate area, chances are that a mile downstream there will be no noticeable change whatsoever in the river's path. Generally speaking, it would take a major engineering effort to actually divert a river so that the point where it eventually empties into the ocean would actually be changed.

It's easy to imagine how that concept can be applied to time. What is the likelihood that the actions of any human being today are going to make one iota of difference to what the earth is going to be like, say, a million years from now? Unless one of us happens to be a scientist about to trigger some unstoppable science-fiction-style subatomic chain reaction which actually destroys the planet, the answer is that any one of us, when we look at the *really* big picture, will likely not divert the river of time at all.

What about the actions of the entire human race? It's easier to imagine how we could actually be diverting the river of time right now so that the planet earth will be very different a million years from now from what it would have been if we hadn't evolved. The permanent loss of major species, and significant changes to the ecosphere will already have created different future paths for our river of time that, regardless of the Gaia force that some say will result in the planet healing itself once we're gone, will be different from the one that would have occurred had we human beings not been around in the first place. Still, no matter what the change in the path will be, there will also be some much more distant point in time near the end of the universe where we can imagine that no matter what we human beings did today, the end of the universe will be unchanged.

The river of time concept is sometimes used to explain historical occurrences as well. If Adolph Hitler had died of a childhood disease, some might suggest that the river of time concept leads us to conclude that some other charismatic madman would have risen to take his place. While the Many Worlds theory allows us to suggest that there must be other universes where that is indeed what happened, it should be clear that this also means that the Holocaust was not an inevitable branch in our river.

So, what we're talking about is in part a question of scale. The turbulence created by our stick or our boulder does create short-term changes in the course of our river. But "short term" is relative. An action could have very limited effects, lasting only minutes or days. "What I Had for Breakfast This Morning" is not likely to change our lifepath for much more than a day or two. However, "What I Eat for Breakfast Every Morning" is much more likely to have a long term change to any individual's path. But will my preferred daily choice between bacon and eggs or fruit salad be likely to change what the earth is like a thousand years from now? The river of time concept says "likely not".

Still, Chaos Theory's celebrated "Butterfly Effect" could come into play with some seemingly minor event, and we could say it represents the opposing viewpoint to this discussion. James Gleick's "Chaos: Making a New Science" introduced many of us to this concept: a butterfly flapping its wings in Tokyo might be responsible for an eventual tornado in Texas. In other words, sometimes a very minor action could be shown to eventually have a major effect, and some seemingly inconsequential action today could create far-reaching turbulence or even a new diversion in our river of time.

Some people have a great deal of trouble with a worldview where all possible pasts and futures really do exist because it appears to eliminate any question of morality–if everything that can happen really does, then what is the point of it all? Interestingly, Bill Murray's character in the film "Groundhog Day" wrestles with this very question. This film, in addition to being a lovely comedy, is also a surprisingly thoughtful discussion of the nature of reality as we are discussing it here. When presented with the same fourth dimensional starting point over and over, Bill Murray's character is given the opportunity to explore some of the seemingly infinite number of fifth dimensional branches available to him from that point. After the initial shock of accepting that this is what has happened to him, he moves through a number of ways of dealing with that idea. He steals. He gets drunk and wrecks stuff. He manipulates others. He decides there is no point and kills himself, over and over again. But eventually, he accepts that the fifth dimensional nature of reality means we each have to take responsibility for our own actions, and the consequences that result.

By the end of the film, he re-enters the world the rest of us live in.[21] We are not experiencing all realities, we are experiencing this one, and a large part of why our current reality is the way it is and continues to be that way is

---

[21] As an aside, we could also use this movie to give us another way of thinking about Feynman's "sum over paths" concept, which tells us there are many ways to arrive at a certain state, all of which could conceivably be the path that was taken, but there is also one particular path that has a higher likelihood of being the one that was taken. At the start of the movie, Bill Murray's character was on a particular trajectory, which made certain outcomes for the rest of his life more likely to occur. After going through the mysterious transformative experience of living the same day over and over, his character finally re-enters the world the rest of us are living in with a new trajectory, making a new set of future outcomes much more likely to occur.

Nine – How Much Control Do We Have?

because of the choices each of us have made and are continuing to make. This is not to diminish the possible negative effects of happenstance or the deliberate malicious actions of others: those factors can and do exist, sometimes to such an extreme that they result in someone's death. We are not trying to say here that the fellow on the six o'clock news chose to be gunned down in a senseless act of random violence, or that a child starving to death on the other side of the planet would have flourished if only they had made better choices. Instead, we are suggesting that the combined choices of a large number of people might have moved us to a different world where criminals could not fire guns, or world hunger had been eliminated. And if more and more people were to see the possibility for change and improvement in their own situation and the situation of the world that is held in the promise of all futures really being possible, it is just a matter of time before we start to move our unwieldy fourth dimensional ship into that direction in the fifth dimension.

However, it's important to remember that the extent of the changes we human beings are able to implement are also limited by the fifth dimension. Until some advanced technology beyond our current imagining allows the fifth dimension to be folded through the sixth dimension, there will always be realities that have to remain on that "you can't there from here" list we have discussed earlier.

Our choices are also limited by the fact that we are all participating in a consensual reality. We've already used this phrase. What do we mean by "consensual reality"? If each of us really are able to collapse a reality out of the tenth dimension through observation, how is there not complete chaos, with each of us on some completely wild acid trip of a life, independent and separate from all others? "Consensual reality" implies that we as individuals must be "buying into" a particular version of reality, agreeing to a certain set of ground rules, a certain common history, our basic "way of seeing the world". Could psychoses such as schizophrenia or severe autism, that affect an individual's ability to perceive the world the way most of us do, be an example of what happens when an individual fails to fully buy into our consensual reality?

In Greg Bear's fascinating novel "Blood Music", he describes a moment where a large group of sufficiently enlightened beings are able to briefly alter the physical laws of the universe and prevent their own demise, simply by altering their consensual reality. If we interpret this through the version of reality we're now exploring, we would say these creatures would have found a way to briefly navigate above the sixth dimension, into the seventh dimension and beyond, momentarily jumping to a universe which resulted from different initial big bang conditions, where the weapon being used against them failed to function because the basic physical laws were different. As a "deus ex machina" this literary device has to be the ultimate, but it is also a fascinating exploration of what the power of consensual reality could be if everyone were to simultaneously agree to change. Clearly, such a high degree of consensual agreement for change is not going to happen amongst human beings any time soon.

As we discussed in chapter five, the quantum observers that are participating in our consensual reality are not just life-forms, but memes, and ways of perceiving the world, and the desire to continue. How much is a fruit fly, an amoeba or a bacterium participating in the creation of our consensual reality? Obviously, the input from a fruit fly is going to be limited to very tiny desires for continuance, and not much more. Even all the fruit flies in the world are not going to be exerting much of a desire for change, because their perception of the universe is so limited. Still, if something were happening in the world that negatively affected all fruit files, one can imagine how their desire for continuance could affect small changes within the limited scope of their awareness. This is how we imagine the very first spark of life potentially being able to choose the fifth dimensional path that allowed it to continue. This is also how ideas like Gaia Consciousness could manifest them-selves: if all modes of awareness on the planet were to simultaneously desire a certain outcome, then that outcome

Nine – How Much Control Do We Have?

is likely going to happen. The advantage that we as human beings have (as would any intelligent race) is that we have the power to imagine and select more wide-ranging and potentially strategic outcomes: a fruit fly simply is not able to perceive the fifth-dimensional timelines available to it in any but the simplest terms, so its reasons for choosing one over the other will be very limited. For wide-ranging systems of belief or perception that are independent of any life-forms, their role as influences in the selection of quantum pathways could also be much stronger than that of our poor fruit fly.

So, in practice, consensual reality tends to be a binding force for each of us rather than a liberating one: there's just too many quantum observers with their own idea of what reality should be, and as a result any really fantastical shifts are virtually impossible to happen at this present time.

In other words, "consensual reality" is why the wonderful options that might seem to be implied through the fifth dimension can be so difficult to achieve. Although each of us has a substantial amount of control, no one person can eliminate world hunger (as one example of many). With the odd exception of the psychopathic actions of a few notable smaller groups or individuals, most huge changes to our world reality require the participation of a large number of people on the planet, all participants in our consensual reality. Some are arguing now that mass merchandising of "brand images" is an insidious way of steering consensual reality on a path that will profit the investors and owners of those brands the most.[xxii] While some may dismiss this viewpoint as paranoia, there is no question that any factor which changes the way of thinking of a large number of people must be significant. With the approach to the dimensions we are now exploring, we can easily imagine how these influences will cause our consensual reality to drift into a different fifth-dimensional path than it would have without that factor's introduction.[xxiii]

Consensual reality is also a tricky concept to deal with because it can be used as a way of excusing oneself from responsibility for the current state of one's life. Everyone has a story they tell themselves of why their life is the way it is at this present moment, and sometimes that story is not completely truthful. It's human nature for each of us to want to put ourselves in a good light. Sometimes that means that we pass the blame on to bad luck or the malicious acts of others, when in some situations each of us should be admitting a certain amount of personal responsibility for bad things that have happened to us. From seemingly small things like "I should have exercised more" or "I shouldn't have eaten that junk food" to much larger acts that seem to be deliberately self-defeating, there is a natural tendency for each of us to say "it's not my fault". Separating into fact and fiction the stories we tell ourselves for why our life is not the way we want it to be is not always easy to do.

For each of us, we will be able to remember moments of malicious, random, or foolish action that could have done us in. It's hard to forget that moment where a large object falling or a silly risk taken might have resulted in our death if we had only been in a slightly different place and time. According to the worldview we're exploring, all of those things did actually happen: that drunk driver you saw last year came over the hill and smashed into you head on, and now you're dead.

And all but the most saintly of us will have moments in our own past where we know we made bad or unfortunate choices, yet we lived to fight another day. Each of us will always have a number of life-paths which could have (and in other quantum realities actually did) result in our death. So how did those of us alive at this instant end up choosing the path where we "dodged every bullet" and are here today, while others, it would appear, have chosen a path where they became another sad statistic?

In other words, if all possible timelines exist, does the person dying of cancer have another version of themselves that avoided the cancer-causing conditions and lived to a ripe old age? And if you are the person currently dying of cancer, should you be asking yourself why you chose that life path rather than another? Clearly, your average terminal cancer patient will tell you they did not choose to have cancer, and would find the suggestion completely offensive. This is a hard issue, wrapped in many conflicting emotions. A simplistic answer might be, the person dying of cancer didn't believe or wasn't aware they had the power to change their life-path, so they didn't–a bitter pill to swallow, and one which fails to take into account the many accidents and diseases which a person could not possibly have known were coming, so any choice which avoided the situation would only have been dumb luck.

This gets back to our discussion of the limitations of the Binary Viewpoint. In simple terms, we can choose a path, or we can choose to not take a path, but there's a third option as well: we can let chance or the actions of others choose a path for us. When we experience pain, injury and serious disease, these tend to eliminate all but the most basic and primal mental processes. Thoughts of higher dimensions and quantum reality (be they conscious thoughts or the subconscious processes we've just imagined) vanish when our attention focuses down to our body's most animalistic desire for trying to find a way to get away from intense pain. We become like the fruit fly, whose role as a quantum observer is limited by its inability to imagine anything but the most simple desires for continuance.

Likewise, depression and illness will tend to close our minds to the possibilities for change that might be still available to us, just when that knowledge might be the most beneficial.

In chapter five we imagined the sixth-dimensional shape which would be drawn by all the possible world-lines for each us. There would be one part of that shape which would represent the version of a person's life which was the longest and happiest, while other parts would represent the versions where they died an untimely death, for whatever reasons. Either through choice, chance, or the action of others, there are those in the current timeline we are experiencing who have ended up on a path where they didn't make it. Clearly, the majority of those persons did not consciously choose the path that resulted in their own untimely death, even if the benefit of twenty-twenty hindsight would now allow them to see the better paths they could have chosen. Some, tragically, may even have appeared to have the most positive, life-affirming viewpoint imaginable, and yet still they succumbed to a terminal disease. So, without for a moment trying to diminish the loss that we all feel when a loved one or a good friend passes on before their time, perhaps we can take some comfort in the knowledge that other timelines exist where those people continue to thrive, even though that's not the timeline we're on. Since we can't eliminate chance and the negative actions of others, our largest responsibility remains to make sure that we as quantum observers have made choices that put us on the path that we, in our hearts, most want to be on.

Despite occasional evidence to the contrary, then, hope for the future and having an optimistic outlook on life–these take on a significant new weight when viewed in terms of each of us being a quantum observer. A defeatist mindset will become self-fulfilling as subtle choices are made in our selection of which fifth-dimensional path we end up travelling upon. Depression, stress, injury and addiction can close our minds to the possibilities of "where can we go from here", and life can become a long dark ladder descending into no future at all.[xxiv] For someone trapped in those realities, this information offers very little comfort, and may even seem irritating or irrelevant, which is unfortunate because that is the situation where an appreciation of the possibilities each of us has opening out before us could be the most useful. You can call it simplistic, but sometimes the simplest things are also the most true: a person's health, a person's career, and a person's life will all be massively affected by whether that person has a positive or a negative outlook. If each of us is collapsing out our own personal reality from quantum waves of indeterminacy purely through the act of observation, then it should be obvious that the choices each of us make will be determined by our own mindset.

Nine – How Much Control Do We Have?

TEN-TRIADS: THE TEN DIMENSIONS REVISITED

Physicists are often drawn to theories that have a certain "elegance": symmetry and simplicity are good things. What we have tried to do here is imagine a new way of viewing reality which can be superimposed over the existing body of knowledge from the worlds of geometry, of Einsteinian space-time, of quantum physics, of superstrings and M-Theory. As simple as this new version of reality may appear to be, we have seen in the preceding pages just the tip of an iceberg of possible questions that could be asked about its implications.[22] Still, as we said at the outset, whether this version of reality has any way to be connected to the mathematics and topologies of string theory is completely outside the scope of this author's ability to discuss. Because

---

[22] For instance: how does sex and sexual attraction fit into this picture? How does this way of viewing reality agree with, and how does it conflict with other spiritual systems? Why are there so many connections between "the role of the quantum observer creating reality" and other philosophical schools of thought through the ages? And the biggest question of all: if the tenth dimension represents the potential for all beginnings and all outcomes for all universes, then have we finally reached "that which has always been and forever will be", or did something/some-body create the tenth dimension?

of that, the only claim we can make here is that this is an entertaining diversion, and a way of exercising the mind with new ways of thinking about how "everything fits together". [i]

So now, let's go back to our original concept of imagining the ten dimensions and explore some more ways of picturing them.

What we have imagined are really only three "triads" of reality stacked on each other, which we can call "triads" because they are each composed of three internal dimensions. We started by simplifying the description of the first triad–the three dimensional space with which we are intimately familiar–into a line, a split, and a fold. By describing the third dimension this way rather than the more traditional "length, width, depth" we set up a pattern which makes it easier to imagine how the other triads can also feel. The three triads, then, would be space (dimensions 1 to 3), time (dimensions 4 to 6), and other big bang universes (dimensions 7 to 9). The tenth dimension would be the aspect of reality described by Kurt Gödel's Incompleteness Theorem, which one can paraphrase to say no system can ever completely describe itself because it can never be outside the system to observe all aspects of itself. The tenth dimension is "outside the system", and any effort to observe any aspect of it immediately collapses a portion of it into the dimensions below. Likewise, in string theory, it is superstrings vibrating in the tenth dimension that create the world we see around us, and the other potential space-times that we can't.

Hopefully it is clear by now that when we collapse out other possible space-times from other initial conditions different from the ones that started our own universe, we end up creating a stack of ten dimensions that are similar in nature but absolutely different and separate from the ones that we are currently in. Three dimensional reality in a world where all the basic physical laws as defined by that world's superstring vibrations and initial conditions (be that a big bang or some other mode of creation) would be completely alien to our own, but there would still be a quantum indeterminacy that would create blossoming timelines of potential in that other universe's second triad, the fourth through sixth dimension (there could also potentially be forms of organized energy in those other universes marvelling at the unlikelihood of the universe they are living in!).

Some will continue to argue that common sense tells us that no matter what universe we are in, time is only one dimension, not three. And certainly, that is true for each person's unique perception of time, because for each of us time feels like a line which extends from our beginning to our end, or from the universe's beginning to end. As we've said over and over in these pages, the common practice of thinking of time as being somehow different from the three dimensions below it could actually be a result of our limited viewpoint, and we are suggesting instead that the fourth dimension is really intimately tied in with the fifth and sixth dimension. The same logic that we use to think of time as being only one dimension could be used to argue that in reality there is only one spatial dimension, the line, and that the three-dimensional space we live in really just represents every possible one-dimensional line that can be drawn.

So, let's look at the concept of lines a little more. We start in dimension one with nothing more than two simple "points". We can imagine that we are on the first point, then we "smear" that point over to the second point, and we can imagine that the line we have formed is actually created by all of the points that lie between. According to Zeno's Paradox, if we were to try to count those points we would discover they were infinite, because no matter how close together one point on the line was to the next, there would always be another point half way between those points. If we view it that way, we can see how an infinity is held even within the lowly first dimension.

When we get to the fourth dimension, we are creating a new "smear" from the dimension below. Here's an example: pick up any nearby object. It has length, width, and height;

it is three-dimensional. Now turn that object on its side (hopefully you didn't choose a cup of coffee for your object!). From the moment right before you picked up the object to when you moved it and turned it on its side, we can imagine viewing this object within the fourth dimension where we would see a long "extrusion" of its shape, with added curves and twists corresponding to the seconds it took you to complete the action of moving the object. As seen from our little window of awareness as a point moving along the linear fourth-dimensional line of time, the object started in one position and was moved to another, and that was the only thing that happened to it. Because we cannot view things fourth-dimensionally, from our perspective the object is still the object, but now it's on its side.

Meanwhile, in the fifth dimension, there is also the moment where you were asked to move the object and you chose not to. From that dimension, we would see a fourth dimensional object which does not move and twist over the same timespan, it just remains in one place. But no matter what action was chosen, the fourth dimensional object created can still be thought of as a "smear" joining what it looked like before you were asked to move the object and what it looks like after you did or did not move the object. Each action/inaction will have created a differently shaped fourth dimensional object. The choice not to move the object might look more like a simple "extrusion" of the third dimensional object if we viewed it across time, while the choice to move the object would have created a more complex looking fourth dimensional object.

(And what if your object were to suddenly, magically, instantaneously return to its original position? Then we would know that time had somehow been "folded" through the sixth dimension to jump us from the fourth dimensional line where we moved the object to the other fifth dimensional branch where we chose not to.)

If Zeno's Paradox tells us that we can imagine even the lowly first dimension as describing an infinity, and certainly the fourth dimension as time can be used to refer to the classical concept of "infinity" what do we need any higher dimensions for? Each triad has its own uniquely self-contained set, and you need to go through the next triad up if you want to get to a different set. What do we mean by this?

Imagine you have a wonderful new camera so big that it can instantaneously snap a holographic picture of our entire universe. Click! Now you have a picture of the third dimension. There is no aspect of time to the picture other than the freezing of an instant. In that picture, all of the possible futures (and pasts) do not exist, all that is represented is that one split second when you pushed the button. If you take a second picture a moment later, things will have changed slightly, but each picture you take is still a snapshot that has no motion, no time element, nothing more than a representation of the third dimension as it currently appeared at that instant.

Now, let's imagine our camera can take a picture of every possible state of our universe, from the beginning of time to the end, not just the outcome we are currently observing but pictures of every possible branch from the beginning to the end, and we put all of those pictures into a gigantic photo album. That photo album represents the second triad, time.

Now, as huge as that photo album is, it still doesn't represent every picture that could have been taken. If there had been initial conditions different from our own big bang, other completely incongruous universes would have been created which would not be compatible with our own, having completely different physical laws and completely different expressions of matter. And, like our own universe, each would have a set of timelines representing all the possible pasts and futures that could have developed within that other universe. If we were to take our camera and create a photo album for each set of beginnings through to endings that each of those initial conditions could have resulted in, each photo album would represent a completely different "space-time" from our own. And if we were to take all of those different photo albums and put them in the back of a moving van, that van would now have inside it the photo albums representing the third triad, "all possible space-times".

And that van, viewed in its entirety, could be thought of as the tenth dimension. Inside that van, we would find represented the three triads, which in descending order would be: all possible universes, all possible timelines within each possible universe, and all possible three-dimensional spaces within each timeline. That's one big van!

Physicists now generally believe that there is a smallest possible structure to the universe, which is known as the "Planck length". First proposed by German physicist Max Planck, it is about 1.6 times 10^{-33} centimetres. Attempting to measure anything smaller than the Planck length breaks down into the world of quantum indeterminacy, where terms such as "length" cease to have any meaning. This implies that there is a shortest possible duration or "Planck time" as well, which is about 5.4 times 10^{-44} seconds, and that would be the time it takes light to travel the Planck length. It seems, then, that in reality Zeno's Paradox does have a physical limit, at which it is physically impossible to continue slicing a line in half. Although it's possible as a mental exercise to continue slicing forever (one half a Planck length, one quarter, one eighth, and so on), it appears that the infinite slices we're imagining in our "smears" we've been discussing may have to always remain imaginary once we get to anything smaller than the Planck length.

If the Planck length is applied to our version of the dimensions, then perhaps we have a way of imagining the potential size of the tenth dimension.

(It should be clear from the outset that all of the calculations we are about to make are, out of necessity, wild approximations. Also, by using the Planck length as our measuring stick for what the smallest divisions could be as we work though our multiplications, we are creating an image which might actually be larger than it needs to be: even though intuition may tell us that quantum indeterminacy, the Planck length, and the Everett's Many Worlds are strongly connected concepts, there is nothing in our theory that demands us to specify that the "next universe over" is only one Planck length or moment of Planck time away. Nonetheless, this should be a useful exercise because it gives us another way to imagine the extravagant multiverse we have based our concept of the tenth dimension upon.)

First of all, let's assume that we really do know how big our current three-dimensional universe is. If we imagine any two points in the fourth dimension, each of those points equals a version of our universe, so the total size of those two points would (obviously) be arrived at by summing together what we know to be the size of the universe at each of those two instants. As we move along our fourth dimensional line of time, each point that we consider adds another universe-sized increment to our calculation for the total size of the dimension.

As we've discussed many times now, our fourth-dimensional line is actually being chosen from the list of possible branches in the fifth dimension. So, if the next fifth-dimensional branch any of us could be moving to is no less than one Planck length (and therefore no less than one unit of Planck time) away from our current point in our fourth dimensional line, then we can already calculate the maximum number of potential points that for any one of us would lead back to the big bang, by dividing 13.7 billion years into its corresponding units of Planck time. Likewise, if we knew how long the universe was going to last, we could divide the time from now until then into units of Planck time. The resulting line would be a certain number of Planck length/Planck time units long, and multiplying those units by the size of the universe at each of those points would give us the potential maximum size of a line in the fourth dimension.

The next calculation is trickier to imagine, because we don't really have a way to know how many potential fifth dimensional branches there could be from this instant (or any other instant) to the one that follows. The number would certainly approach infinity, but we know it doesn't reach infinity because there are always branches on our fifth-dimensional path which we can describe as being on the list called "you can't get there from here". Whatever number approaching infinity that we would care to plug in here would be multiplied by the already unimaginably large number we had arrived at for the size of the fourth dimension, and that would give us the size of the fifth dimension.

Arriving at the size of the sixth dimension then requires us to estimate all of the points of view or memes that might be circulating around our universe, collapsing the quantum wave into classical reality, from the big bang to the end of time. Once again, this would be a number approaching infinity. How many different ways can reality be experienced? We might as well ask how many grains of sand there are in the universe. All we can do is make a good guess, multiply that by the number we had from dimension five, and that gives us the size of dimension six.

For dimension seven, we then have to imagine how many different universes there could be, starting from different initial conditions and creating physically incompatible realities from the one we're currently in. Again, this would be a number approaching infinity, which we multiply the previous number by to get the size of dimension seven. How many different ways could the basic physical laws of each of those universes change over the course of their development? We have evidence now that our own universe appears to have subtly changed its constants over time, this would be a path that our universe moved through in the eighth dimension (even though it continues to feel like a point in the seventh dimension from our perspective). Multiply the number of possible paths for every possible universe by the size of dimension seven, and there is the size of dimension eight.

As with dimension six, dimension nine fills in all of the "you can't get there from here" paths that each of the eight-dimensional lines we have just imagined would need to complete our picture of reality. Remember though, that even in the ninth dimension, the role of the quantum observer still comes into play. How many different points of view would there be collapsing out different realities from the tenth dimension to create those ninth dimensional shapes? Intuition tells us here that there are probably substantially fewer memes at this level because these would be the "big picture" memes rather than the multitude of tiny viewpoints that can manifest themselves in the lower dimensions. A monotheistic viewpoint might even suggest that there would only be one quantum observer at this level, or perhaps very few.[23] In any case, we pick a number for the number of ninth dimensional quantum observers we choose to believe there would be, multiply it by the number we had arrived at for the eighth dimension, and there we have the size of the ninth dimension.

In our initial analysis, we said that viewing the entire ninth dimension as if it were a single point would be the tenth dimension. Even having said that, it may still be a surprise to now understand that the tenth dimension, and the ninth dimension in its entirety, must both be the same size.

Let's return again to the idea of each new triad starting with a dimension formed from a line which "smears" the triad below. We create the first dimension by joining one point to another. Thinking of it that way, we could define those "points" as being in the dimension below the first dimension, and say that they are in "dimension zero". Since these points have no size, they are just pointers indicating particular locations, this can be a useful starting point for our discussion. Following that logic, then, the first dimen-

---

[23] This could be a discussion topic for all you Marvin Minsky fans out there: if we are imagining the mind of God, would we be seeing one single viewpoint, or would we encounter something similar to human consciousness? In other words, would God be a "Society of Mind" just as human beings are?

sion is created by joining two points from the "dimension below".

Likewise, the fourth dimension takes the dimension below as if it were a single point and "smears" it to another point (representing the dimension below in some other state) to create another kind of line, and we think of this line as being time.

This means when we arrive at the seventh dimension, it is the bottom of a third triad, which is different from the first two triads we've just imagined. When we first explored the seventh dimension we suggested that it can be interpreted to represent our traditional concept of infinity/eternity. But that is only part of the story, because all of the possible infinities for our universe would only be a single point in the seventh dimension.

The other point that we would most likely be drawing a line to in the seventh dimension would be the collected timelines of some other completely different universe from ours, one that started from different initial conditions. Since those initial conditions are defined as we enter reality from the tenth dimension, we could say that each "point of entry" becomes the endpoint of a line that can be drawn in the seventh dimension. The two points we join in the seventh dimension could be any two arbitrary universes, and an observer travelling along a line in the seventh dimension would be sliding (or "smearing") through the infinities of adjacent universes, each created by incremental changes in the initial conditions that led to each universe. Like the bifurcations of chaos theory (as explained so well in James Gleick's previously mentioned book, "Chaos"), some of those adjacent universes would seem predictably similar, while other adjacent universes would suddenly jump to completely different states as some line or threshold is crossed by the initial conditions.

With the evidence that even our own universe's basic physical constants may have changed slightly over its history, we must also be imagining that our universe has travelled upon a short line in the seventh dimension, chosen from some other possible lines it could have drawn in the eight dimension, and that all the possible lines our universe could have drawn would be creating a shape in the ninth dimension. We know that the seventh dimensional line we have travelled on so far must be a short one because the constants have only changed slightly. We also know that if the universe had travelled much further along that line that our basic physical laws would have changed too much for our universe to continue in its current state, since most of those constants that our universe is constructed from have very small windows of tolerance. As we have said before, if those constants change very much, we know we would then no longer be here to ask the question of how we came to be in such a finely tuned universe in the first place.

The "line" seems like such a simple concept, but that simplicity is deceptive. In the first triad, which is three-dimensional space at any one specific moment in time, any two locations can be connected by a line. Think about how profound that thought really is: no matter what point you can imagine in the known universe, you can draw an imaginary line from yourself to that location, which will join those two locations within space, completely independent of time.

Now imagine this: if we were to look through a telescope at a nearby star–say, one ten light years away–and imagine ourselves drawing a line to what we're seeing, that line would actually be to the star as it existed ten years ago. Clearly, what we're looking at through the telescope is not what the star looks like now (even though the two views might be very similar), because of the time it took for the light from that star to get here. So, if we're wanting to imagine that we're drawing our line from ourselves to that star within the first triad only, then the line we want to draw will not be to what we currently see through that telescope but what we're going to see through that telescope ten years from now! To say it another way, the line we want to imagine ourselves drawing should be independent of time, because we want to draw it only within the first triad.

But suppose we did decide we wanted to draw a line from ourselves to what we currently saw through the telescope? Since what we're seeing through the telescope is from ten years ago, we would have to draw a line that joins two points across the second triad, which is time.

Keeping the first triad separate from the second in our minds can sometimes be tricky, since the part of our awareness that is attached to our physical bodies is always moving forward along a line in the fourth dimension. Imagining three dimensional space as a timeless slice works fine if we compare it to the idea of a photograph, but in life there is no way for us to actually freeze time, which is what we would have to do if were to actually be existing in the third dimension only. So, even as we look around and tell ourselves we are three-dimensional creatures, we are constantly moving from one three-dimensional slice to the next, and those slices are continually joining one to another to create a four dimensional line. In a process which is essentially invisible to us, we believe ourselves to be three-dimensional (that is, living within the first triad), but we are constantly moving within the fourth dimension (the second triad), and ultimately all of our possible lives are creating a shape in the sixth dimension.

After all this discussion, there may still be those who have followed the concepts presented here but who will say this system doesn't need to go higher than six dimensions, because the sixth dimension viewed in its entirety represents infinity for our universe and that's all there is. Let's try to imagine a description of the second triad that makes the reasoning behind this clearer.

No matter what possible past or future for our universe we might imagine, we can fold through the sixth dimension to instantaneously jump from any point in our current timeline to another completely different timeline that could have or will have occurred in our universe. But there are still timelines which are not part of any possible past or future reality for the universe we live in because those timelines start from different initial conditions. To jump to those we have to move into the third triad. To put it another way, in the second triad we are always in a specific snapshot of the time-space that was generated by the initial conditions of our big bang, and to get to any other snapshot we have to enter (or fold through) a higher dimension than the second group of three.

The third triad is admittedly the most difficult to imagine because its complexity makes it the most alien to our way of thinking. As we've explored, navigating in the third triad is to be navigating through or across one infinity to another, or to be moving within universes where the basic physical laws are changing.

We should now take a brief detour to make note of some of the mental shorthand tricks we have used throughout this discussion–for instance, the concept of the "fold" only applying to the third, sixth, and ninth dimension. In reality, no matter what dimension you are in, it is always relevant to imagine the next dimension up is what you would fold through if you were to want to instantaneously jump to someplace else in your current dimension. This, like the concept of each new dimension being at right angles to the one below, is very easy for us to visualize within the lower dimensions (try it and you'll see), and becomes increasingly difficult to visualize in the higher dimensions.

Likewise, limiting our concept of the first, fourth, and seventh dimension as being lines which somehow treat the dimension below as a point, and which "smear" the point to create the dimension above, is certainly convenient for the picture we are imagining. However, in many senses it is also an unnecessary restriction. We can easily visualize this in the lower dimensions but it applies to all of them: a first-dimensional line can be extruded out to create a second dimensional plane, which can be extruded out to create a three-dimensional object, which can be extruded out through time to create a fourth dimensional shape, and so on.

Clearly, using "line, branch, fold" was a useful way of trying to provide a mental image of how each dimension can be built upon another, and helped us to mentally organize the dimensions into their triadic structure. While that triadic structure is very important to keep track of, it should be remembered that in reality each of those concepts can be used to climb up from one dimension to another. That is to say, no matter what dimension we are looking at, it's always valid to say we are going to use a line, branch or fold to get to the next dimension above.

Interestingly, we tend to conceptualize each triad from the bottom up. That is to say, if we are creating a mental image of what three-dimensional space is like, we generally imagine it as the first dimension, leading to the second, leading to the third: length, width, depth. To imagine three dimensions in reverse order is much more difficult, because of how much we are paring away from the possibilities. In other words, distilling the concept of a simple line from the infinite space of our universe is a gigantic conceptual leap that is inherently more difficult than it is for us to imagine how three lines at right angles to one another can be extended to result in infinite space. The same is true for the other triads. Conceiving of time as it is expressed in the sixth dimension and working down to our linear experience of time in the fourth dimension is much more difficult than the concept of imagining the line, branch, and fold that are the fourth, fifth and sixth dimensions. In the third triad the problem is even more extreme: because of this it's much easier for us to imagine that when we collapse reality from the tenth dimension, we enter it as a point in the seventh dimension through initial big bang conditions, and that the eighth and ninth represent branches and folds through the other possible universes generated by other initial conditions.

Even though we have just shown how the line, the branch, or the fold can each be used as a way to get from any arbitrary dimension to the next one above, there are still many ways in which keeping the line, branch and fold assigned to their position within each triad can be helpful.

By doing so, we can imagine the correspondences between the three layers of each triad. This gives us a shorthand way of thinking which becomes more useful as we ascend to the higher dimensions.

In other words, dimensions one, four, and seven have correspondences because they are each at the bottom of a triad, and this is true for the other related dimensions of each triad as well. Hopefully, those correspondences are fairly clear by now, but let's look at them again.

The first, fourth, and seventh dimensions are all lines joining two points. Those points can be widely separated or right on top of each other, which is why it's also so easy for us to think of these particular dimensions as being points rather than lines. This is quite self-evident in the first dimension. In the fourth dimension, we often tend to think of time as being a point rather than a line: "the eternal now"[24] which is our conscious mind experiencing reality from moment to moment. The seventh dimension can be thought of as a line that joins all possible times for our universe to all possible times for some other universe. But since we exist in only one of those seventh dimensional points, it is also easier for us to imagine the seventh dimension as a point rather than a line, which is valid in the same way as our tendency to sometimes think of dimensions one or four as being single points is equally valid.

The second, fifth, and eighth dimensions are all branches that represent a potential splitting off that, in the dimension below would be impossible to conceive of. In other words, it's quite possible to travel on a branch in the dimension below and be unaware of the twists and turns we are making in the dimension above, just like the Flatlander on the Möbius strip. So, branches in the fifth dimension continue to feel like a straight line when experienced in the fourth dimension; and the small line our universe may have travelled on, even though it was selected from the available

---

[24] Or, as Timothy "Speed" Levitch in Richard Linklater's fascinating film "Waking Life" calls it, "The ongoing WOW".

possibilities in the eighth dimension, has created what appears to us to be only a seventh-dimensional line.

The third, sixth, and ninth dimensions are where we can imagine a fully-realized shape that is described by all of the lines and branches that are defined in the preceding two dimensions. A person's third dimensional body is a shape defined by the lines and branches of the first and second dimension. In the sixth dimension, a person's "shape" is defined by all the lines and branches that their life could have taken in the fourth and fifth dimension. And the shape of our own unique universe in the ninth dimension describes all of the possible drifts in the basic constants that could have occurred over the history of our universe, which are lines and branches in the seventh and eighth dimension.

Let's review just a few more of the ramifications of all this.

When we say that the first dimension is a line, that line is free to exist anywhere within the third dimension. Likewise, our fourth dimensional line of time could exist anywhere within the sixth dimension. The same holds true for the seventh and ninth dimensions. This is a tricky concept to hold on to, because it can sometimes mislead us into saying that the fourth dimension is equivalent to the sixth, and so on. If we are to avoid this confusion we have to keep in mind the following three concepts: within each of the three triad sets, a line can occupy any of the three positions in its triad; a branch can occupy the middle and higher positions in its triad but not the lowest one; and a fold can occupy only the highest position in its triad.

This concept also applies to points, because of our tendency to sometimes conceive of the first, fourth, and seventh dimensions as being points only. Any first-dimensional point we can conceive of can be located somewhere within the third dimension. Any fourth-dimensional point in time we care to imagine will be located someplace within the sixth dimension. And any seventh-dimensional point containing a specific universe and all its possibilities will exist someplace within the ninth dimension.

We have often have spoken in these pages about time, the fourth dimension, being a way to join two points in the third dimension. But sometimes it is not always clear in those discussions that "the third dimension" is not an independent dimension, it is really a triad of the first three dimensions, inseparably joined together into what we call "three dimensional space". With that in mind, it becomes easier to imagine how time could also be the next three dimensions, inseparably melded together into a line/branch/fold triad that directly corresponds to our first triad in concept and function.

Ultimately, there is a "feeling of completeness" contained within each triad, which is what helps us to imagine how a triad can be like a point when you view that triad in its entirety from the dimension above. Here is an interesting corollary to that idea: the tenth dimension has its own unique "completeness" because it contains the potential for a triad of triads.

In chapter six, we touched upon the idea that groups of three would become more important as we neared the end of this text. At that point we were discussing how dualistic viewpoints can often lead to a third viewpoint in which the first two are perceived simultaneously, or as a whole. We see this concept intuitively in the third dimension: if we think of the first dimension as a line and the second dimension as a branch, we have established a binary/dualistic viewpoint. Then, by adding the "fold" of the third dimension, we have established a way to consider the lines and branches of the first two dimensions in all their possible configurations. In other words, the third dimension gives us a holistic viewpoint of what is much more limited when viewed from the first and second dimension. From the third dimension, we easily perceive all the intermediate steps that would be moved through as a second-dimensional line is folded.

The idea that sometimes the third, simultaneous viewpoint is automatically implied when we consider the first and second viewpoint can be applied to many concepts. Still, it should also be clear that there are times when the dualistic viewpoint is describing two things which are truly incompatible opposites, in which case the only third layer which could be implied is "neither". Duality in string theory and quantum physics is so interesting to us because it does seem to indicate that there are many times that we can describe our reality as having three states: "state one, state two, or simultaneously state one and state two".

As nonsensical as the equation "one plus one equals three" actually is, we can use that phrase as a "mental slap" to startle our brains into remembering this important concept.

We've already looked at how the line, branch and fold can work no matter what dimension you start from, and that the particular assignments we gave them were partly just for the convenience of our exploration. While the triads we've looked at do have strong arguments for being considered with the groupings we have put forth in this text, even triads can sometimes be useful when applied to other dimensional groups of three.

For instance, if we think of our third dimension as being the base of a line/branch/fold triad, we have a way to incorporate Kaluza's original concept from way back in 1919, which said that the basic structures of our reality are defined at the fifth dimension. Brane Cosmology tells us that our universe's particles and forces (with the exception of gravity) are "trapped" on a three-brane where parts of the tenth dimension's strings are embedded. If we think of the line/branch/fold possibilities that could be defined by those particles and forces, we get to Kaluza's fifth dimension. We could even say that our own possible future branches are trapped within this same fifth dimension, because the sixth dimension contains only the "can't get there from here" branches of our universe that are inaccessible to us until we invent time travel or wormholes. Coincidence? Quite probably, but an interesting coincidence nonetheless.

There have also been some interesting theories advanced in Brane Cosmology which indicate that the three-brane and the seven-brane are the two most stable configurations out of the ten dimensions, and that perhaps it is the interaction of the strings embedded in these two branes which are creating our universe. Since, in our version of reality, the seventh dimension is where the current basic physical laws for our universe are defined, this also seems like an interesting coincidence.

Whether these connections really exist between leading-edge theories of physics and the tenth dimension as presented in this book is, as I said at the outset, not something I can even hope to prove. I can, however, state the following two facts: my theory of reality is based upon there being ten dimensions, and string theory also says that our reality occurs from the tenth dimension. In the end, this may be the hugest coincidence of all the coincidences we have examined. Still, I believe that intuition will tell some readers that the two ideas are strongly related, and ultimately that is all I can hope for as we work our way through these ideas.

In one sense we have reached the end of our journey now, but there is still one final part of this mystery I would like to explore.

Ten – Triads: The Ten Dimensions Revisited

ELEVEN–INTERFERENCE AND CONNECTIONS

Let me start this chapter with a bit of background. When I first conceived of this book, it was my intention that it have ten chapters: ten dimensions, ten chapters, it all seemed neat and tidy. Even when it became clear to me that the most recent writing about string theory tends to focus on there being eleven dimensions rather than ten, I doggedly clung to the implications within those discussions that in some senses the tenth and the eleventh dimension are equivalent.

Then, when I showed a draft of this book to Larry Bauman (a good friend and a talented writer and filmmaker), we had some stimulating conversations which ended with him saying "Okay, I can see your argument for how parts of what I believe I am experiencing are really just shapes in the higher dimensions. But I still found myself by the end of the book wishing that there had been more of a conclusion. If all this dimensional stuff is what's happening, then what should that all *mean* to me?"

This chapter is my response to that question.

When we imagined the possible pasts and futures that the second triad holds for our universe, we drew the conclusion that moving through those points is really "just geometry": all of those potential points exist as per Everett's Many Worlds theory, and it is the quantum observer collapsing those realities through the act of observation that makes any one of those realities decoherent from all of the others.

Back in chapter five, do you remember how we imagined that our reality is created from two interlocking webs? There is the web of physical reality as we experience it down here in the third dimension: the multiple branches possible for that physical reality can be viewed in their entirety as shapes within the sixth dimension. When we imagined a person's physical body in the sixth dimension, we described it as a shape which would be thickest where it is drawn from the most likely world-lines, but which would have feathering and tiny threads representing the other less likely paths that individual's life could also have taken.

It can be easy to forget, though, that this sixth-dimensional shape is not some airy concept that is essentially disconnected from our experience: the physical body each of us are now living within is, at any moment, a fourth-dimensional cross-section of that overall sixth-dimensional shape.

Because our physical bodies are what we are locked in as we directly experience the third and fourth dimension, it is very important that we remember that all of the following discussions are rooted from our experience as physical creatures with minds that are living inside organic bodies. As stimulating and inspiring as it can be to imagine the many parts of our awareness that are dividing and floating around in the dimensions as we have imagined them,[25] there is still the hard truth, which is that during our lifetime we have to keep coming back to the body we were given at

---

[25] This would include our discussions of out-of-body experience, meditation, clairvoyance, ghosts, reincarnation, hallucinogens and the many similar metaphysical and "fringe science" concepts we have looked at in various chapters throughout this book.

Eleven – Interference and Connections

conception. If we are truly imagining that a part or all of our awareness has left the body forever, then we must be talking about death, diseases of the mind, or simply a part of our meme-system which has ceased to associate itself with our physical body and which is therefore no longer a part of our experience as the physical creatures that we are.

Still, it is useful to our discussion to think about the other parts of reality which we are not currently experiencing as physical creatures. We have already discussed how there are corresponding shapes representing the meme-systems that follow each physical body around, helping to give it the feeling of being a unique personality. We know that over time and geography different memes rise and fall in popularity, sometimes shared by many people and sometimes by only a few. We also know that different memes are often assumed and discarded by individuals over a lifetime. Because of this we know that most of those meme-systems would have completely different overall shapes in the sixth dimension from the sixth-dimensional bodies they were sometimes attached to. As a result, we can imagine that viewing moments of radical shifts in the way of thinking of a large population would be very interesting from this particular vantage point.[26]

---

[26] We touched on the following idea in chapter eight, but it bears repeating: when we looked at the idea of dark matter being gravitational leakage from the adjacent physical universes available to us within the fifth dimensional branches, we mentioned the idea that the number of available branches from one moment to the next does not change. This is relevant to our current discussion as well: when we think of meme-systems that must have more interesting textures and discontinuities at certain moments because some event has caused a larger number of people to change their way of thinking, we must be careful not to assume that at that moment there has been a change in the number of fifth dimensional branches available to us from our current fourth-dimensional line. The fact that more people from the general populace take the next, most likely branch certainly adds to its significance from our perspective, but we know that the perceived amount of dark matter does not fluctuate up and down at these moments of significance, so the other available branches must still be there and be just as real. What will be changing with the shifting meme-system shapes is the likelihood of any one of those upcoming available branches to be selected by our consensual reality. But even our consensual reality will have feathering and tiny threads spinning off from the central mass representing the other less likely paths which could have been taken, and which at any particular moment *were* actually be taken by some parts of the overall group of quantum observers.

Eleven – Interference and Connections

We must remember, though, that if there is no observer then there is only the indeterminate wave of possibilities contained within Everett's Universal Wavefunction, which we have come to know as the multiverse. As long as we are imagining a universe that has a specific beginning and ending, then there must be parts of the system of quantum observers we are also imagining that extend back to the beginning and out to the very end of our universe. In the third triad, those observers can extend well beyond even those limits to encompass all the other physically incompatible universes as well.

It may appear, then, that if we imagine a particular meme that has existed since the perceived beginning of our universe, collapsing a specific version of reality out of the wave of potential universes through the act of its observation, that we are imagining an aspect of the Creator-God. But there is a second way to view this puzzle. Could the feeling of "self" that each of us holds within us also be "just geometry"? In other words, what if this interlocking web of memes were exactly like the interlocking web of physical realities implied by the Many Worlds theory? This would mean that the potential for all ways of viewing the world, and the potential for all the different systems that we think of as being our own soul, are also held within an indeterminate wave of potential at the tenth dimension that has always existed, and will always exist.

According to that version of reality, then, we are all Schrödinger's Cat, not just physically, but spiritually as well. Physically, we are simultaneously observing and not observing the reality that currently surrounds us, and this reality is only one of the many that we could potentially be observing. As meme-systems or souls, we are also simultaneously both our own point of view and potentially all other points of view as well.

Wow, it doesn't get much more cosmic than that, does it? This would appear to be the "time is an illusion and we are all one with the universe" concept taken to its ultimate conclusion. What this seems to deny, though, is that there is still something mysterious about how our own consciousness and our own physical reality is not just part of the "all", it is one very specific cross-section out of the white noise of possibilities contained within the tenth dimension.

Some might assume that it is our intention here to arrive at an atheistic viewpoint where we have no need of a Creator because the potential for reality and awareness to exist have always been contained within the tenth dimension. Are we really suggesting that the magical spark of life that animates a living creature is an illusion, nothing more than a geometrical shape held within a higher dimension? In the same way that we have wrestled with imagining the incredibly extravagant universe of matter and physical reality, it is equally mind-boggling to try to conceive of the mystery of life and awareness being nothing more than lines and textures in a higher dimension.

What we're looking for, then, is a way to explain the profound experience of self-awareness and life within the context of the system we have imagined. We need something that seems to spring unbidden, which can exist across multiple dimensions, and which we can clearly feel its absence when it leaves a living creature. Personally, I am drawn to the idea of interference patterns when we discuss these issues.

Many of us will recall our high school physics classes, where we saw two interlocking waves in a ripple tank create a pattern which appears as if by magic. Some readers might be more familiar with this effect as the moiré pattern, which can occur when any repetitive visual pattern is superimposed over another, and is particularly vibrant when one or both of the patterns is moved around. Be it a ripple tank or a moiré, in either case a new pattern appears which is a result of the interaction between two other layers. In some cases this effect can be quite startling, as the new pattern appears to have an independent life of its own, appearing, moving, and disappearing as the source patterns are changed.

Eleven – Interference and Connections

The pattern that is generated in a ripple tank is the result of two opposing effects: there are places where the intersecting waves cancel each other out and both become invisible, which is "destructive interference". But what we are interested in here are the places where the two intersecting wave patterns are reinforcing each other, through a process which is called "constructive interference".

In this book we arrived at two interlocking sets of patterns which we could also think of as being created from waves of probability: a physical system, and a system of memes. The mysterious spark of "self" that each of us carries within us, then, would be like these interference patterns: a pattern that results from the interaction of those two waves, and which changes as those wave patterns change. Is the interference pattern we see in the ripple tank or the moiré pattern really there? As long as the waves are there, it certainly would seem to be. But as soon as one of the wave sources ceases to interact with the other, the interference pattern disappears. "That which ceases to change ceases to exist" works so well as a concept for life and consciousness, then, because it says that when there is no interaction between those two interlocking patterns, we return to indeterminacy.

Like the other groups of three "triads" that have appeared in this book, this would be one more: a feeling of "self" as the unique third layer which springs as an interference pattern or moiré pattern from the interaction of the two other layers we have imagined.

Just a few pages ago we described the tenth dimension as containing a "triad of triads". Now we extend that concept yet again.

As soon as any aspect of the tenth dimension is examined, we fall into the nine dimensions below. We started by examining physical reality, which is in nine dimensions, divided into three groups of three. We then added a meme-system which is freely moving across those three groups of three in the same nine dimensions. And now we add the interference patterns that are created by the interaction of those other two layers, creating in total a dimensional reality that we could think of as being three groups of three tall, and spread across three different systems (the physical, the meme, and the interference systems).

As we built our layers, we kept building groups of three, perceiving the resulting triad as a single point and then creating a new group of three from that starting point. Now that we have imagined a third layer which is the set of potential interference patterns resulting from the interactions between those other two layers, we are supposing that these would also be expressed in different ways across the different dimensions. And yet at the tenth dimension, that cloud of possible "selves" that could be expressed in those interference patterns would still be there as potential only, waiting to be collapsed out into the dimensions below.

This gives us one more way to think about why the tenth dimension has a different quality to the ones below it. Not only is it a "triad of triads" from the physical layer, and from the meme-system layer, this effect would be happening from the interference pattern layer of consciousness as well. We can see here how the "three becomes one" concept that we've used again and again in building our dimensions continues to recur, but always seems to finish at the tenth dimension. Is God the tenth dimension? For those of a spiritual mindset, it is very easy to imagine that the tenth dimension must be where God emanates from, or that this is the place in which He/She rests between Creations.

By the time we arrive at this image of triads and interference patterns, there are interesting parallels to Juan Maldacena's "universe as a hologram" concept which could bear further exploration—but that's a whole other discussion.

It should be apparent now that the quantum observer that we have referred to throughout this text is embodied in this idea of interference patterns. We don't have an "observer" until the indeterminate wave of physical reality and the indeterminate wave of the meme-system interact, through the process of constructive interference. The added wrinkle that we are adding now is an important one: in the preceding chapters we have always imagined meme-systems as being something that chooses to interact with the indeterminate world of quantum physics. Now we are saying that the "observer" is a layer that results from an interaction between these two other systems.

It's important to realize here that we are not imagining that only one interference pattern results from this interaction. Just as the physical system and the meme system have many ways that they can be collapsed, the resulting interference pattern will change depending upon the content, and the angles of intersection between those other two layers. So, if we imagine a line drawn in the fourth dimension of the physical layer, we can see how that line can be used to represent our concept of time. As we move on a point along that line, this can give us the causal connections we are familiar with, such as chemical reactions that are always expressed as "A plus B always equals C". As we imagine the meme-systems that can interact with that point moving along that line, we have all the ways that life and consciousness can result in the different physical realities that can be experienced. In other words, even when we limit our viewpoint in the physical layer to a very specific window, there are still a nearly infinite number of ways that the physical reality can be experienced in the interference patterns that result from those interactions.

Does this solve the problem of how free will fits into our system yet? Haven't we just moved the quantum observer's choices from an indeterminate wave of possibilities in the meme system over to an indeterminate wave of possibilities in the constructive interference system? We'll get back to this question in a few pages.

For now, let's ask this question instead: how is choice manifested in the third triad? If we imagine points in the seventh dimension that represent the infinities of universes, and branching lines in the eighth dimension that represent universes with different basic laws or universes that have changed their laws during their existence, then in the ninth dimension we are imagining rounded shapes that are being drawn by all those potential lines. In the same way that we human beings can imagine branching timelines that for each of us would be creating an overall shape representing our body's potential pasts and futures in the sixth dimension, there will be shapes in the ninth dimension that represent the different potential infinities of the different universes springing from different initial conditions. Some of those ninth-dimensional shapes might be like the sixth dimensional shape of the possible lives of a fruit fly: even when we imagine the most fortuitous, longest-lasting version of some different-initial-condition universes, the possibilities for continuance are limited by that specific universe's initial conditions (we've discussed this idea a number of times: some universes immediately collapse upon themselves, others explode into entropy with no apparent organization, and so on).

We have imagined each person having a version of their possible timelines in the sixth dimension that represents their longest and happiest life. Even if that particular life might be a tiny thread in the sixth dimension because it is so unlikely, it would be there nonetheless. In the ninth dimension, our own universe must also have a version of itself where it flourishes the most, and lasts the longest.

Consider this: until the end of our longest-surviving universe, there could be observers and memes that are still collapsing the wave of indeterminacy for that physical version of the universe, and there will be a world-line that is the most likely (but not the only) way for our universe to have gotten there, right from the big bang to whatever the end of our universe holds for us.

So, we are back once again to Feynman's "sum over paths" concept from chapter four: it tells us that at any moment, there are many ways that a particle could have arrived at its current position, even though there is just one that is the most likely. Since we are imagining a system of memes that has the same simultaneous wave/particle nature as the physical world does, we are proposing that Feynman's concept applies not just to the particles but to these memes as well. When we imagine the longest-lasting version of our own universe, then, we are also imagining that there is a "sum over paths" for a set of memes that exist now, and also exist at that point in the most-distant future, and that therefore there is a most likely path that gets us from now until then.

We can also imagine that there could be new memes that rise in popularity at the end of our universe because of the specific conditions of that unique time period. These are not as interesting to us right now because there would be no "sum over paths" line of probability that gets us from those future-memes back in time to today, because those particular memes would not be in effect at this current part of our universe's history. What we are interested in right now are those memes which are dominant today and which would continue to be influential at the end of time. By definition, then, these longest-surviving memes would be the ones that have the potential to get us to the longest-lasting version of our universe. We know this because in the view of reality that tells us time is not a one-way arrow, those memes are the ones that have already gotten us there.

We can also surmise that there must be a certain set of big-picture memes that have existed since the beginning of our universe, extending all the way back to where our version of reality was first made decoherent from the others by observation. This means that there must be a certain set of "biggest-picture-of-all" memes that have been exerting an influence right from the beginning of our universe until today, and some or all of those memes could continue to be active right to the end of the universe.

Let's explore what those biggest-picture-of-all memes might be. We already touched on this idea in chapter ten: the memes that are most influential in the third triad would be much more general than the memes expressing them-selves in the lower triads. For instance, the meme that says

"I prefer gravity over no gravity" would be important in the third triad, while the meme that says "I prefer the Beatles over the Rolling Stones" would be meaningless.

When we look at the extremely unlikely universe the anthropic priniciple tells us we now happen to be in, we can draw some conclusions about which memes have been more influential so far. Memes that prefer life over no life, continuance over destruction, creativity over repression, innovation over failure, and order rather than entropy would appear to have the upper hand when we think about the version of our own universe that has survived since the big bang, and which we are living in today.

Likewise, when we imagine the version of our universe that lasts the longest, it's easy to imagine how those memes we've just listed might be the ones that continue to have a strong influence to the end of our longest, most happy universe. However, since there is no guarantee that we will remain on that particular path to the most fortuitous version of our universe's future, there could also be other memes of destruction and disorder that will have their own strong influence and eventually gain the upper hand within any one specific timeline.

Sadly, like the person who dies before their time not because it was their desire to do so, there will be versions of our own universe where the ultimate desires for continuance do not win out. To believe otherwise puts us back in the world of Novikov's Consistency Conjecture, which tells us that we have no choice but to proceed down a certain path, unable to change our future because it will preserve its own self-consistency at all costs.

Somewhat strangely, this appears to be the answer to our question about free will then: the fact that each of us do not automatically ride the world-line that takes us to the best possible version of ourselves is proof that free will exists.

For our universe, we already know that some extremely unlikely choices have been made in the selection of the basic laws for the universe we are in. Is this evidence for an expression of free will in the third triad?

Eleven – Interference and Connections

In the third triad, we find the other physically incompatible universes which physicists have told us must also exist. These are the universes in which other big-picture memes will have risen to dominance, and there would be particular universes for which certain memes will have a strong affinity. Like the child who takes joy in knocking over a tower of blocks, or a person taking joy in blowing things up or shooting them, there would be a universe just made for the memes that prefer destruction over creation. There would also be universes where very little changes over eternity, and the memes that are drawn to stability at all costs would naturally tend to interact with those physical universes. The fact that our consciousness tends to block out things that don't change would seem to be a clue about how much the "stability at all costs" meme holds sway in the universe we are living in at this moment.

In our discussion of the anthropic viewpoint, we suggested somewhat in jest that conspiracy theorists should love its implications. Now we're looking at an interpretation where we're giving that idea some more weight: there really are other universes where other big-picture memes have "gotten their way". To the extent that any conspiracy can also be looked at as being just a description of the chain of events that led to a certain outcome, we can apply that same thinking to our own universe that we're in, and to the other universes we're not.

Does the interference pattern we see in the ripple tank control its own results? Clearly, it does not.

But the lovely thing about the term "constructive interference" is that it gives us a second way to think about this concept: we can view consciousness as the moiré pattern that springs unbidden from the interaction of two patterns that exist in the ninth dimension and below. Or we can imagine that the pattern that we are experiencing as reality and mind is actively selecting its own pattern as it chooses to cause the meme system and physical system to interact: in other words, the pattern is choosing to "constructively interfere" as it create its reality. This offers us the possibility that there are parts of our own consciousness that would be actively trying to select a path which, in the biggest picture of all, has the potential to move us towards the version of our universe that lasts the longest and flourishes the most.

This also offers us the possibility that for each of us, there are parts of our consciousness which know what the longest, happiest personal life path for each of us will be, and those parts will be trying to exert their influence to draw our life towards that conclusion. While the mitigating factors we have already discussed—chance, the actions of others, consensual reality, and so on—will also be exerting their influence, this part of our own consciousness must also be part of the picture. In many cases, those potentially negative factors will have conspired to move each of us away from our own best possible world-line: but no matter what has happened so far, each of us must still have a version of ourselves that from this moment forward will be the one that makes the best of their current situation and lives the rest of their lives in the happiest, most fulfilled way available to them. When each of us looks into our own hearts and is honest about where we are in our own life, each of us should ask this question: am I listening to the part of me that I know will move me towards the best possible version of myself from this moment forward?

So, this means we end our discussion with one more choice: we can choose to believe that our quantum observer is an eternal spiritual force, an "unseen eye" which gazes upon itself and marvels at the miracle of life as we experience it. Or we can choose to believe that our unlikely universe just happens to be the one that we, as a part of the potentially infinite fabric of the tenth dimension, currently and spontaneously believe ourselves to be experiencing (in other words, our feeling of "self" is a result of processes that are essentially "just geometry"). With either approach, the end result is the same, and one is no less mysterious than the other.

Eleven – Interference and Connections

Philosophers have wrestled with this quandary through the ages, and in these modern times people are again returning to ask the same enduring questions. What am I? Why am I here? Is there more to reality than what I see around me right now? With the incredibly, extravagantly detailed layers of reality that we have just imagined at the tenth dimension, the unique and beautiful world we live in becomes just that much more fascinating.

Eleven – Interference and Connections

AFTERWORD

Each of us has our own way of viewing the world. Each personal viewpoint, while unique and special, also shares much in common with others, and that is what connects us to other lives across space and across time.[xxv]

When I was seven, I remember a day at the end of June where I was running across a field and my foot dropped into a small hole, probably made by a gopher. I don't remember now if I actually stumbled and fell, but I have a strong memory of what I felt as I was wrenched down without warning–that at the moment the universe somehow shifted. Over the next few years, as I tried to puzzle out what had happened to me at that moment and why it felt so significant, I gradually began to imagine a "splitting off" that might have happened at that point–that there could be other worlds that now exist where I took a much nastier fall, perhaps ended up in a wheelchair, possibly even died. The idea that I had ended up on one of the more fortuitous paths at that moment out of the many that could have occurred (and, as I later came to believe, actually did occur) became the seed from which the viewpoint described in these pages grew.

Ultimately, this text is a personal expression. Like any other person's viewpoint, there will be things contained within these pages that for some might resonate strongly, and to others might seem of little relevance. What I find fascinating about the way of viewing the world we have just explored is that there is room for a huge number of viewpoints within. Each is just another way of collapsing reality out from the tenth dimension, and the fact that one viewpoint seems alien or incompatible to another is just another example of how multi-faceted and finely textured the possible ways of expressing reality can be. How strange and wonderful is the world we live in![xxvi]

INDEX

THE SONGS

As I said in the introduction, this project began as a set of songs. The idea of "concept albums" has always appealed to me, and as a songwriter I have created several over the years. After I finished writing these songs in 2002, I found that the difficulty with my idea of a "concept album about the nature of reality" was that it still left too many ideas that I was thinking about unexplored and unexplained. For a while, I was thinking that I would write a booklet that would be included with the CD to help the listener understand my point of view. As you can see with the book you are holding now, that little booklet I was planning took over, to the point that, quite frankly, the songs have become somewhat secondary to the project. Still, who knows, maybe this will all end up being part of an "Imagining the Tenth Dimension" theatrical play or movie some day!

When I wrote these songs, they were based upon the idea that seven dimensions is as far as you need to go to account for all aspects of the universe, which was my belief for the last couple of decades. Then, in spring 2005, it occurred to me during a trip Gail and I took to Australia that there was an additional triad I could add that would take me to the tenth dimension, and I immediately became fascinated with how that seemed to tie so nicely into string theory's tenth dimension. Still, I probably would not have been able to write this book if I had not ended up in June 2005 with blood clots on my lungs. I spent almost two weeks in the Cardiac Surveillance Ward at Regina's Pasqua Hospital as the doctors tried to figure out what was wrong: eventually they decided that the clots had started in my legs as a result of sitting on the plane too long during my trip Down Under. During that two week period, as I lay in my comfortable hospital bed, in an environment where the ward's wonderful hospital staff worked so hard to make sure I was happy and comfortable, I wrote all of the first draft of this book on my trusty laptop. Then, I spent the following ten months researching and refining, adding many of the scientific references that are in these pages now.

In the 1980's and early 1990's, I was music director and composer for the Globe Theatre here in my home town of Regina, Saskatchewan, Canada. During those years I composed dramatic underscores and created soundscapes for a great many productions. I also collaborated from time to time with the Globe's playwright-in-residence, the very talented Rex Deverell on some satirical musical comedies. Three of the songs listed in the following pages were created for a 1986 play of Rex's about how people in difficult circumstances can turn to fascism as the possible cure for their problems: this black comedy's unlikely-sounding title was "Resuscitation of a Dying Mouse".

In some of the shows on which we worked together (with me as composer and Rex as playwright) Rex would write the song lyrics or he would give me a set of words that I would rework into a song. Other times I would write the songs in their entirety, and that is the case with the three songs from "Resuscitation" showcased in the following pages. Even though these songs are all my lyrics and my music, I would still like to acknowledge the conversations Rex and I had that led to these songs being created for that production. By asking me to write songs about big-picture ideas such as the nature of conspiracy, and what draws people into making certain choices, he helped me to begin giving voice to the ideas I had been carrying around in my head about how the world fits together. Ultimately, these ideas were already part of the multi-dimensional way of thinking that I am describing in this book. Thank you, Rex, for encouraging me to think about these ideas more clearly as you questioned my philosophy: twenty years later, I still believe that "everything fits together".

[i] EVERYTHING FITS TOGETHER

(originally written for Globe Theatre's Resuscitation of a Dying Mouse, 1986)
(revised and updated June 22 2005)

It's the age old question, it always stays the same
People turnin their eyes up to heaven and callin out names
Some may get an answer, some may turn away
When they don't want to know too much, cause it's easier that way
Hidden back between the pages, written in between the lines
There's a spider's web of connections there for you to find

Cause everything fits together, you may not see that now
But there'll come a day, when you'll see the way
There's always a why and a how
Everything fits together, it's all part of the show
Soon there'll come a day when you'll see the way
And you'll know (there's a reason why, there's a reason why)
And you'll know (there's a reason why, there's a reason why)
There's a reason why, there's a reason why
There's a reason why you feel the way you do
There's a reason why you do the deeds you do
There's a reason why you feel the needs you do
There's a reason why, there's a reason why
(There's a reason why, there's a reason why)

In this world of wonder, in this world of pain
In this world of mysteries that still remain
There's a hunger growing, we all would love the chance
To see the hidden strings that sing to make it all dance
Just when you thought the universe couldn't be any more complex
You started climbing up through the levels, one to the next

Where everything fits together, you may not see that now
But there'll come a day, when you'll see the way
There's always a why and a how
Everything fits together, it's all part of the show
Soon there'll come a day when you'll see the way
And you'll know
Everything fits together (everything fits together)
Everything fits together
Everything fits together (everything fits together)
Everything fits together

ii SEVEN LEVELS

Paul announced it with a gleam in his eye
Timothy found it a-written on high
Sanskrit mystics, chakras too
Everybody says it so it must be true

There are seven levels, levels to the universe
Seven levels, from seven down to the first

First comes the point, a singularity
Impossibly small, as in geometry
No width or depth, a place to start
Imaginary construct, the very first part

Then comes the line of first dimensionality
The simple way from point A to B
The second is a branch, from one line to another
A splitting apart, it's easy to discover

There are seven levels, levels to the universe
(move through 2 to travel to a 1)
Seven levels, from seven down to the first
(fold through 3 to jump to another 2)

Three is the curve, three's our space
The world we live in, everything and every place
Now you find when you fold the lines
A to B is shorter, they can even collide!

And four is time, a line so narrow
Past to future, straight as an arrow
The simple way from one day to the next
A journey taking us from birth to death

There are seven levels, levels to the universe
(move through 4 to travel to a 3)
Seven levels, from seven down to the first
(fold through 5 to jump to another 4)

Five is a branch or a split in the line
Back to the future, a wrinkle in time
And this is how it's always gone
We choose from five for the four we're on

The Songs

Cause there are seven levels, levels to the universe
(move through 5 to travel to a 4)
Seven levels, from seven down to the first
(fold through 6 to jump to another 5)

Six is the space we'd have to move through
To change reality: if we wanted to
Live in the world where JFK
Was never murdered, six'd be the way

And seven is all, a singularity
Simultaneous, every possibility
Every yes and every no
Eternity, infinity, impossible to know

There are seven levels, levels to the universe
(seven is infinity a formless bore)
Seven levels, from seven down to the first
(things get interesting here in four)
There are seven levels, levels to the universe
(seven is infinity a formless bore)
Seven levels, from seven down to the first
(things get interesting here in four)

iii BURN THE CANDLE BRIGHTLY

Each of us carries it within us
Each of us has a little spark
That moves us to dance in the sunlight
That lights our way through the dark

I want to burn the candle brightly
Never let it fade
Burn the candle brightly
Let it light my way, yeah, yeah

Each of us tends to a fire
That burns so dim or so bright
Some like a blaze in all its glory
Some like a flicker in the night

I want to burn the candle brightly
Never let it fade
Burn the candle brightly
Let it light my way, yeah, yeah

Some go gently to the darkness
Some will rage to the end
All of us carry it forever
This tiny spark that we tend

So when this journey is over
And that beautiful spark is finally gone
We can see that the vessel is empty
But we know that the light carries on

I want to burn the candle brightly
Never let it fade
Burn the candle brightly
Let it light my way (let it light my way)
I want to burn the candle brightly
Never let it fade
Burn the candle brightly
Let it light my way (let it light my way)
Every day

iv THE UNSEEN EYE

(In the distance we hear children, repeating a strange little skipping song out on the playground:)
("All we are is a point of view
It makes me *me*. It makes you *you*.
Quantum waves are many things
Until we *view* them, then they *spring*
Into our world as what we see
It makes you *you*, and it makes me *me*")

In the universe of all universes
Anything is possible
Everything has happened, and will happen again
In the universe of all universes
Grey and formless
Till you choose a point, to become the first -- when
You can think of it as data
This dark and shapeless void
Unrealized potential
In the static and the noise
Till in the universe of all universes
The unseen eye
Opened and collapsed the wave, and we entered on in

Now we know it's the act of observation
That gives the world its how and why
So the big bang is just an illusion
It's just the opening of the unseen eye

Now any single point that we choose for entry
Leads to a long chain
From the very first yes, or the very first -- no
All the laws of physics, all the rules of nature
Defined in an instant
By the very first choice, or the dice we throw
Though Einstein objected
To imagining a God
Who gambles for Creation
The thought was just too odd
But deep within us in every living creature
There's a connection
To this shared consensus, of the world we know

Cause we know it's the act of participation
That gives the world its how and why
So the big bang is just an illusion
It's just the opening of the unseen eye

The Songs

And the missing dark matter that binds the universe
The mysterious mass that science cannot find
Is in the many worlds of possibility
That are just around the corner in time

Now the universe of all universes
If the truth be known
Is an awful bore, viewed as a whole
But just a tiny shard viewed from any angle
Reveals complexity
It reveals such beauty, reveals a soul
So does it make a difference
How we got to what we see
If it's really just coincidence
It's still a wondrous thing

And we know it's the act of observation
That gives the world its how and why
So the big bang is just an illusion
It's just the opening of the unseen eye
And the unseen eye, is you and I
And the unseen eye, is you and I
And the unseen eye, is you and I

^v AUTOMATIC

Musta been runnin on automatic
I simply can't recall
How did I get here, what was I doin?
No clue at all
Lost my place in the conversation
What were we talking about
Thought I was here, must have been dreamin
Without a doubt

Automatic
Automatic
Automatic
Musta been runnin on automatic

What was for breakfast, just this mornin
I really couldn't say
Out there circlin another planet
So far away
Where was my head at, was I drivin
Not even seein the road
Was I only goin through the motions
Don't even know

Automatic...

Julian Jaynes showed me he had the answer
In the bicameral mind
Conciousness broken down into pieces
Oh what a find
We've all been runnin on automatic
Since we were back in the trees
But still we made it here on automatic
How can it be

Automatic...

Something beautiful and complicated
Does it ever seem strange
How we could do that on automatic
Hard to explain

Automatic
Automatic
Automatic
Musta been runnin on automatic

^{vi} CONNECTIONS

Connections in time
Connections in space
Connections we share with the whole human race
Back to the very first chemical chain
That started it all, one thing remains
It's all about connections

Just another sappy love song
Climbin to the top of all the charts
Go ahead and ridicule it
You can say that it's not art
But what's inside that formula
That lets it touch so many hearts?
How could those recycled cliches
Grab so many from the start?

Connections in time...

Shared beliefs, and strong emotions
Connections of common family bonds
Draw us all together
They help to make us strong
This system of thoughts and memories
The "I" inside that I call me
There are parts I share with others here
Now and back through history

Connections in time...

Past life regression
Trips to the psychic fair
If time is an illusion
Then those other lives you share
Parts of them could be right here
Writing the books you love so well
Singing the songs that touch you deeply
Your reincarnate self

Connections in time...

I think I met myself today
I think I saw my eyes
Another me in another body
Livin another life

The Songs

vii NOW I LAY ME DOWN TO SLEEP

Now I lay me down to sleep
To rest my weary head
If I should die in slumber deep
Remember what I said

It's not the end of the world
It's not the end of the dream
It's just the end of a body
Not the end of a soul

So what am I so afraid of?
A little bit of sorrow?
It all continues flowing on
The past into tomorrow

Now I lay me down to sleep
My journey finally through
A list of things undone, unsaid
So much left to do

So what am I so afraid of?
The thought that this has ended?
Did I try my best to be
The person I intended?

It's not the end of the world
It's not the end of the dream
It's just the end of a chapter
Turn the page and move on

Now I lay me down to sleep
To rest my weary head
If I should die in slumber deep
Remember what I said

^{viii} BIG BANG TO ENTROPY

I slowed down
Till I heard the moon
I heard the moon ringing
Ringing like a bell

I slowed down
Till I felt the earth
I felt the plates sliding:
Skaters on a pond

And I finally felt the long groove moving underneath
Births and deaths of galaxies pounding out the beat
And I finally heard the whole song at once:
Big Bang to Entropy
Big Bang to Entropy
Big Bang to Entropy

I slowed down
Till I saw the sun
I saw the sun spinning
On a pinwheel's arm

And I saw the long chain of our DNA
Stretching back to the beginning for so long
And I saw the mighty ocean that surrounds and sustains
Connecting us together in a song

I slowed down
Till I saw the song
Was only one of many
One of many more

And I finally felt the long groove moving underneath
Births and deaths of galaxies pounding out the beat
And I finally heard the whole song at once:
Big Bang to Entropy
Big Bang to Entropy
Big Bang to Entropy

It begins as nothing, silence at the end
Every song's the same after or before
But the parts in between, there are so very many forms
More than we could ever hope to know

^{ix} SENSELESS VIOLENCE

(for Globe Theatre's Resuscitation of a Dying Mouse, 1986)

Senseless violence (Senseless violence!)
Crime in the streets (Crime in the streets!)
Don't talk to strangers (Don't talk to strangers!)
Or people you meet (Cause they could be just as dangerous!)
These are dangerous times that we live in
These are dangerous times that we live in
Senseless violence (and you can't get away)

All the latest atrocities on the six o'clock news
Everybody's cranin their necks to see the view
And you are too
Somebody killed a cop parked at a roadside restaurant
Somebody went crazy pulled out a gun
Shot up the place, just for fun

Senseless Violence (Senseless violence!)
Crime in the streets (Crime in the streets!)
Don't talk to strangers (Don't talk to strangers!)
Or people you meet (Cause they could be just as dangerous!)
These are dangerous times that we live in
These are dangerous times that we live in
Senseless violence (and you can't get away)

You got your foot on the brake
Cause you can't take your eyes off the car crash scene
You're all movin so slow, wonderin who it might have been
It's a little obscene
When you see the need to feed upon such butchery
Get some popcorn and coke and find a seat
It's solid entertainment on the silver screen

Senseless Violence (Senseless violence!)
Senseless Violence (Senseless violence!)
Senseless Violence

^x ADDICTIVE PERSONALITY

Now it's really only natural
It's always been the same
That when something makes you feel good
You want that something again
But when that something starts to hurt you
And you just can't let it go
And you wake up feelin poorly
But you wake up wantin more

Addictive personality, Addictive personality
Addictive personality
Addictive
Personality

Is it nature, is it nurture
That got you to this place
Where you're tradin your tomorrows
For what you're trapped into today?
Is it the constant inundation
Of the media machine
Is it the way that you were brought up
Or just something in your genes?

Addictive personality, Addictive personality
Addictive personality
Addictive
Personality

Every day is a new day
Every day you're back to one
And today can be the new day
When you say you're finally done
Or you can find some more excuses
That today will be the same
Cause it's easy to continue
When you say you're not to blame

Addictive personality, Addictive personality
Addictive personality
Addictive
Personality

xi THE ANTHROPIC VIEWPOINT

(This song combines the concept of the "Anthropic Principle" as advanced by Stephen Hawking in his "The Universe in a Nutshell" with Gödel's Incompleteness Theorum, one of the central points of Douglas Hofstadter's amazing "Gödel, Escher, Bach", and throws in some strange ideas of my own. And it's got a good beat and you can dance to it.)

Pay no attention to the man behind the curtain
The only thing that I know for certain
In everything that you say and do
The only thing you know for sure is you
Believe in that and you will be okay
You could live to fight another day, some day

Pay no mind to those tiny little voices
Every day you gotta make some choices
Make 'em right and you can carry on
Make 'em wrong and you will soon be gone
And if it seems just a little unfair
Get used to it, cause the stars don't care, don't care

In the anthropic viewpoint
The reason we're here is because we're here
And if it were impossible
Then we wouldn't be

If there's other worlds then we've just missed 'em
No way to know what's outside our system
We're like goldfish livin in a bowl
What's beyond it we can never know
All we can do is theorize
Cause we can never... get outside, outside

In the anthropic viewpoint...

So here we are in the Hydrogen Conspiracy
That's the way that it certainly appears to be
What's the reason, where's the rhyme
How'd we end up on this line
All those other possibilities
They're just as real, but they don't have me
It's no big deal, not worth a fuss
They're just as real, but they don't have us, have us

In the anthropic viewpoint
The reason we're here is because we're here
And if it were impossible
Then we wouldn't be

xii THE END OF THE WORLD

The end of the world
Oft predicted, never realized
The end of the world
Never here, it's such a surprise
How could millions be so wrong?
The end of the world
The end of the world
Has already been, it's come and gone

Looking back through history
We oft encounter prophecies
Of end times so very very near
Next year, five years, ten from now
A state of flux, some way somehow
The process of postponement never clear

The end of the world...

With space and time a continuum
Of everything that is to come
And might have been, in one infinite ball
Multiple timelines, now I see
Apocalyptic destinies
Prophets proven prophets after all

The saucers?
Already landed
Our star bodies?
Already attained
Y2K? The global pandemic?
Huge disasters
The big freakin' asteroid?
Destroyed the world

The end of the world
Oft predicted, never realized
The end of the world
Never here, it's such a surprise
How could millions be so wrong?
The end of the world
The end of the world
Has already been, it's come and gone
The end of the world has come and gone

xiii BLIND FAITH

Isn't it incredible?
This beautiful, crazy world that we're livin in
Seems so impossible
That only dumb chance
And blind happenstance
In a clumsy cosmic dance
Collided and created this all

To be an evolutionist
You gotta have faith in a force that's so mystical
Pulling strings behind the scenes
You believe it directs
Creatures one to the next
And it's never perplexed
When the form that's between couldn't stand a chance

Same boat, different oar
Same sea, nothing more
If this is a creation, then there must be a Creator
Blind faith can say the question is resolved
But if there's a Creator, how was He created
Blind faith can say that God just evolved
And round and round the whole thing revolves

Where's it all comin from
You can follow the cause and effect through eternity
Evolved or created?
You must still reach a spot
When you connect all the dots
That the first thing you've got
At the start is just something that "is"

Same boat...

Isn't it incredible?
This beautiful, crazy world that we're livin in
Seems so impossible
That only dumb chance
And blind happenstance
In a clumsy cosmic dance
Collided and created this all

Same boat, different oar
Same sea, nothing more
If this is a creation, then there must be a Creator

Blind faith can say the question is resolved
But if there's a Creator, how was He created
Blind faith can say that God just evolved
And round and round the whole thing revolves

^{xiv} I REMEMBER FLYING

I remember flying
Flying so high
I'd push off from the ground
And push into the sky
I would leave the surly bonds
Of gravity behind
I remember flying
From some other time

I remember floating
Ascending to the clouds
Achieving elevation
Then descending to the ground
I remember thinking
It was natural as can be
To be up there floating

I remember moving
In languid slow motion
Like some giant creature
Deep in the ocean
Flying, diving, swooping, soaring, climbing, looping, laughing...

I remember flying
From so long before
And I think that there will come a day
I'll be flying once more
I remember flying
From more than my dreams
I wish I was flying
Right now

The Songs

^{xv} WHAT WAS DONE TODAY

All the tiny little hurts, All the sad little tales
All the wounds that turned to scars That never went away

All the evil in the world, All the bad turns of fate
All the ignorance and sloth That never let things change

They steal something precious
They open up a hole
In the lines of possibility
To keep us from our goals
They steal something precious
I see it drain away
Tomorrows that can never be
Because of what was done today

Now if all things are possible
It still must be clear
Because of chance or circumstance
Sometimes you can't get there from here

And it's nice to have your wishes
And it's great to have your dreams
But for a starving child in Africa
They hardly mean a thing
How can they mean a thing?

We've all got something precious
A wondrous tiny spark
That drives us to continue
And to fight against the dark
But they're stealin something precious
I see it drain away
Tomorrows that can never be
Because of what was done today

Big Money
Can't hear you
Big Power
They don't care
Big reasons
To change the system
Revolution's in the air

xvi TURQUOISE AND WHITE

A dream of turquoise and white
Water and sand
A dream of fragrance and light
You take my hand
A dream of warmth and water
Suspended in the air
My tropic getaway
I'm there

A dream of laughter and sun
Swimming in blue
A dream so languid and soft
I turn to you
A gentle breeze, a whisper
A day without a care
My tropic getaway
I'm there

Turquoise and white, I close my eyes
And see it in my mind
Turquoise and white, a melody
A calm and peaceful time

A dream of turquoise and white
Water and sand
A dream of fragrance and light
You take my hand
A dream of warmth and water
Suspended in the air
Our tropic getaway
We're there
We're there
We're there

xvii CHANGE AND RENEWAL

Water of life, flow through me
Water of life, renew me
Water of life, surround me
Water of life, astound me

Every minute of every day
I keep changing, I keep changing
Nothing ever stays the same
All replacing, rearranging
Every cell that's in me now
Was not the same when I was born
In an endless constant flow
Renewing when they're old and worn

Every minute of every day
We are water, we are water
Swimming in an endless sea
Mothers, fathers, sons and daughters
Molecules of H-2-O
That move around and move between
In an endless constant flow
Connecting us in ways unseen

Change and renewal
Incarnations
Change and renewal
Inspiration

Every minute of every day
All around us, all around us
There's a sea of new ideas
Waiting out there to astound us
Innovation coinciding
Simultaneous discovery
Flowing out there, waiting for us
Just as easy as can be

Change and renewal
Innovation
Change and renewal
Inspiration

The Songs

Every minute of every day
Pay attention, pay attention
Open up to what's around you
Endless paths to new invention
When you hit a roadblock
It's as easy as can be
You can drink a glass of water
Find a new idea

Change and renewal
Imagination
Change and renewal
Inspiration
Change and renewal

Water of life, flow through me
Water of life, renew me
Water of life, inspire me
Water of life, rewire me
Water of life, surround me
Water of life, astound me

xviii FROM THE CORNER OF MY EYE

From the corner of my eye, I saw it
Thought I caught a glimpse at the edge of sight
Just a tiny inkling
Very hard to see
A flutter like a thousand wings in flight

In a corner of my mind, I questioned
How could there be more than this world of ours
Just a trick of vision
Disorder of the mind?
A pattern of tiny twirling stars
At the corner of my eye

From the corner of my eye
I saw the dance and spin
Of other worlds within
Such a mystery
From the corner of my eye
Hidden in the folds
Those other worlds untold
How can it be

In a corner of my heart, I felt it
There's so many worlds that we cannot see
Just around a corner
Hard for us to turn
Angels dancing endlessly
At the corner of our eyes

From the corner of my eye
I saw the dance and spin
Of other worlds within
Such a mystery
From the corner of my eye
Hidden in the folds
Those other worlds untold
How can it be

xix POSITIVE VIBES

Positive vibes, I will be sending
Positive vibes your way
Sure can't hurt, and it just might help
To send you positive vibes - every day

And isn't it a mystery
How it all goes together
Looking back through history
Have you ever wondered whether
When a country falls
Or somebody succeeds
What was causin it all
Was it just their deeds?
Or was there something more in behind?

Positive vibes, I will be sending
Positive vibes your way
Sure can't hurt, and it just might help
To send you positive vibes - every day

Not tryin to get all mystical
But I've always had a suspicion
That there's more than just the physical
Hidden in the composition
Of the things we do
What we think and feel
I believe it's true
I believe it's real
That we can help to make things all right

With positive vibes, I will be sending
Positive vibes your way
Sure can't hurt, and it just might help
To send you positive vibes - every day

There are things that we can never know
There are places we can never go
There are things we have to just believe
And this is what works for me:

Positive vibes, I will be sending
Positive vibes your way
Sure can't hurt, and it just might help
To send you positive vibes - every day

The Songs

XX HANG A LEFT AT THE LIGHTS

As you're headin down your highway
You know you gotta read the signs
You gotta watch the other drivers
You gotta stay between the lines
You gotta listen to your wheels
Cause they'll tell you bout the road
You gotta watch out for distractions
And think about where you're goin

Maybe it's time to hang a left at the lights
And choose another way
Maybe it's time to put on the brakes
Cause sometimes it's okay
To hang a left at the lights

Are you writin big fat cheques
That your body just can't cash
Burned your candle at both ends
Well it's never gonna last
Are you surfin on the top
Or are you draggin in the dirt
Are you headed for a fall
Are you headin for some hurt

Maybe it's time to hang a left at the lights...

Gimme that roadmap, where the hell's that star sayin "you are here"
Gimme some directions, this time try to make 'em clear

Time for a tuneup
Time to change the oil
Top up my fluids
Check my sparks and coil
Thanks to the pit crew
I'm ready for another lap
But this time will be different
If things start to turn to crap

I'll be sayin maybe it's time to hang a left at the lights
And choose another way
Maybe it's time to put on the brakes
Cause sometimes it's okay
To hang a left at the lights

xxi MAKING IT UP AS I GO

I'm just making it up as I go along
Making it up as I go
Sometimes I'm right, sometimes I'm wrong
But I keep making it up as I go along

Never been slow with an answer
Even when I didn't have a clue
I'd go with what my heart told me
Usually I'd muddle through

I'd plow so brazenly forward
Never lacked for confidence
With just my first gut reaction
Some kind of common sense

And I'm still making it up as I go along
Making it up as I go
Sometimes I'm right, sometimes I'm wrong
But I keep making it up as I go along

Some people say it's the bible
Some people say it's the mind
Some think it's technology
That will finally show the sign

Point me in the right direction
Tell me which is the way
How will I know if my life is blessed
By the path I choose today?

I'm just making it up as I go along
Making it up as I go
Sometimes I'm right, sometimes I'm wrong
But I keep making it up as I go along

xxii INSIDIOUS TRENDS   (Aug 23 82)
(on the Rob Bryanton album "Alcohol and Other Drugs", 1983)

Step right up and try a few
These ones sure look good on you
Take one home and try it for a week
They're the very latest fashion now
You can do without'em but I don't know how
And of course they carry our money back guarantee

Yes there's always somethin new
Tryin to get a hold on you
Yes there's always somethin new
Tryin to sink its teeth in you

You can see it on your TV set
You can hear it on the radio
You can play it on your stereo
And you probably will (you know that you will)
And in every magazine and paper
They'll play you the same old song
It's big and new and made for you
And it's the best thing to come along

Yes there's always somethin new
Tryin to get a hold on you
Yes there's always somethin new
Tryin to sink its teeth in you

They will break down your resistance
Like they were breakin down a door
They'll just hit you again and again and again
Till you can't take no more (you'll give in for sure)
It's a million dollar gamble for a billion dollar prize
Who can keep you the latest on the longest artificial high?

(Instrumental with collage of commercial clips/hype)

Hey!

Yes there's always something new
Tryin to get a hold on you
Yes there's always some big deal
Sayin nothing else is real
Yes there's always something new
Tryin to get a hold on you
Yes there's always something new
Tryin to get a hold on you

(Step right up and try a few
These ones sure look good on you
Take one home and try it for
They're the very latest fashion now
You can do without em but I don't know how
And of course they carry our money back guarantee)
Money back
Money back guarantee, money back
Money back guarantee, money back
Money back, money back

Oh, insidious trends are creepin through my life
Insidious trends are creepin through my life
Insidious trends are creepin through my life
Insidious trends are keeping me alive

^{xxiii} SECRET SOCIETIES

(for Globe Theatre's Resuscitation of a Dying Mouse, 1986)

I believe in secret societies and underground confederacies
That move in my life
I believe in sisterly sororities and brotherly fraternities
And they're part of my life

And there are signals, and there are signs
Right before us all the time
But we stumble deaf and blind
Cause we never realize

There are wheels that turn, that we never see
There are eyes that are watchin you and me
There are tears people cry cause they'll never be free
Trapped in the arms of a secret society

I believe the guy sittin next to me waits for a sign from me
To show him I know
What he needs, or maybe what I need from him, but he won't ever let me in
It's a common tableau

Yes it happens all the time
We're all sendin out signs
Cause we all need to know
Who are friends are, who's the foe

Cause there are deals that are struck that play with our dreams
And there are people who move in places unseen
And pinocchios who dance as if they live and breathe
Tugged from above by a secret society

Oh, I believe it's true

xxiv SEE NO FUTURE

You see no future on the road that you've been travelin
You see no reason to continue any more
Still you keep on keepin on
Cause it's the way you've always gone
Won't you tell me what the hell you do it for

Now if there's one thing I can say – it's you're consistent
And you're persistent to a fault, sure, some'd say
Are you stubborn or just dumb?
Why don't you try to find someone
Who will help to turn you round the other way
When you see no future

No tomorrows
Just todays
Is that the way you wanna stay?
No wishes
No dreams
Can't you find another way?

I wish some happiness could join you on your journey
I hope that fortune finally finds you on your way
But tell me how will you ever win
When that big wheel that you're in
Has you runnin the same circle every day
You see no future

No tomorrows....

You see no future on the road that you've been travelin
You see no reason to continue any more
Still you keep on keepin on
Cause it's the way you've always gone
Won't you tell me what the hell you do it for
When you see no future
When you see no future
When you see no future
When you see no

xxv WHAT I FEEL FOR YOU

Much greater minds than mine
Have tried to figure out
The secrets of the universe
And what it's all about
Masters of the abstract
Seekers of the spell
That fits it all together
I know the quest so well

But it all keeps coming back
No matter what I do
The only thing that's real for me
Is what I feel for you

And what I feel for you
Is what makes me carry on
My world would be so pointless
My reality so wrong
The secret gears and levers
That spin behind the scenes
To make what's here before us
Must only do one thing

Cause it all keeps coming back…

Much greater minds than mine
Have tried to figure out
The secrets of the universe
And what it's all about
Masters of the abstract
Seekers of the spell
That fits it all together
I know the quest so well

But it all keeps coming back
No matter what I do
The only thing that's real for me
Is what I feel for you
The only thing that's real for me
Is what I feel for you

xxvi THANKFUL

In this improbable world
In this impossible life
At the end of infinite happenstance
Leading back to the big bang

I am thankful for what I have
I am thankful for what I've been given
I am thankful for those I love
And for this life I'm livin

And in the multitude of paths
That could have ended before now
I am grateful for the unseen hand
Which led us here somehow

I am thankful for what I have
I am thankful for what I've been given
I am thankful for those I love
And for this life I'm livin

The universe is beautiful
More complex than we can believe
And praisable for what it holds within
A tapestry of threads
That each of us must weave
From each and every moment that we're in

In this improbable world
In this impossible life
At the end of infinite coincidence
Leading back to the big bang

I am thankful for what I have
I am thankful for what I've been given
I am thankful for those I love
And for this life I'm livin

About the Author

Rob Bryanton made his first record at twelve, and was host of a regional CBC-TV music series at twenty. He is the President of Talking Dog Studios (www.talkingdogstudios.com) in Regina, Saskatchewan, Canada, which specializes in music and sound for film and television. He has been nominated nine times in the last nine years for Canada's prestigious Gemini Awards, four times in the category "Best Original Music Score for a Dramatic Series", and five times for "Best Sound for a Dramatic Program". Recent projects to which Rob has contributed his talents as a composer and sound mixer include the hugely popular CTV series "Corner Gas", and two CBC-TV mini-series "Prairie Giant: The Tommy Douglas Story", and "The Englishman's Boy". Rob is also responsible for the theme and underscoring on CBC-TV's "Canadian Antiques Roadshow".

While Rob has had poems and song lyrics published in several anthologies over the past decade, "Imagining the Tenth Dimension" is his first book. It represents the culmination of a life-long fascination with science, philosophy, and the nature of reality, which (as he tells in these pages) began at the age of seven. Rob is also the current President of the Saskatchewan Motion Picture Association, and is an active volunteer in his community. A typical stubborn prairie boy, he is proud to have built a career for himself as a composer and sound mixer in his home town, and to have been a part of Saskatchewan's burgeoning film and television industry for the past 30 years.

Rob lives in Regina with his wife Gail and their dog Buddy. Gail and Rob have two sons, Todd and Mark.

"The same logic that we use to think of time as being only one dimension could be used to argue that in reality there is only one spatial dimension, the line, and that the space we live in just represents every possible one-dimensional line that can be drawn."

                (Imagining the Tenth Dimension, Chapter Ten)

"In my personal opinion, this is the most exciting confirmation that the ten dimensions as we are imagining them here could truly be connected to the structure of reality – in this context, dark matter has a simple and clearly understandable explanation. All we have to do is accept that time is a spatial dimension rather than a quality that we overlay on the other dimensions."

                (Imagining the Tenth Dimension, Chapter Eight)

The Songs